SCHOOL IS NOT A
FOUR-LETTER
WORD

SCHOOL IS NOT A FOUR-LETTER WORD

How to Help Your Child Make the Grade

L o u A n n e   J o h n s o n

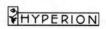

New York

Library of Congress Cataloging-in-Publication Data
Johnson, LouAnne.
School is not a four-letter word : how to help your child make the
grade / by LouAnne Johnson.—1st ed.
p.   cm.
Includes bibliographical references (p.   ).
ISBN 0-7868-8312-X
1. Education—Parent participation—Handbooks, manuals, etc.
2. Home and school—Handbooks, manuals, etc.   3. Child rearing—
Handbooks, manuals, etc.   I. Title.
LB1048.5.J65   1997
649.68—dc20   96-46150
CIP

Book design by Chris Welch

FIRST PAPERBACK EDITION

10   9   8   7   6   5   4   3   2   1

AUTHOR'S NOTE

The incidents in this book are true and the people are real, but all names have been changed to protect the privacy of my colleagues, my students, and their families.

To one who bears the sweetest name
and adds a luster to the same,
who shares my joys,
who cheers when sad;
the greatest friend I ever had.
Long life to her, for there's no other
can take the place of my dear mother.

—author unknown

CONTENTS

Chapter 1

WHO AM I?

The first time a parent called to ask me for advice about helping her handle her teenage son, I did my best to provide intelligent, reasonable suggestions. After I hung up the phone, I remember thinking: *How can I, a woman with no children of her own, advise this person who has raised three active, healthy children? Who am I to offer advice to anybody—especially parents?* Before I decided to write this book, I posed those same questions to people whose opinions I respect—a vice-principal at my high school, two former college professors, the chair of the education department at a local university, a few fellow teachers, several current students, and, of course, my mother. My mother said, "Go ahead, dear, but be sure you wear a sweater if you're going to sit for long periods at your desk." My colleagues and professors reassured me that my education, experience, and success in the class-room made my advice valid. But it was my students, con-fiding in me via their private journals, who convinced me that this project was worthwhile.

"I know my parents love me," one girl wrote, "but they don't always listen to me like you do. And you still re-member what it's like to be a kid. It's like you never grew up." (I'm not sure if her last comment was a compliment, but I took it as one.)

My favorite response came from a boy who had earned miserable grades in English before being assigned to my class. "You liked me just for me, even if I didn't get good grades, and nobody never, ever did that before."

Liking students in spite of their behavior isn't always easy. But it is that ability to separate the person from the action that has enabled me to reach so many "unreach-able" kids. I believe in one thing above all else: *People, particularly children, do what they think they have to do to get what they want or need at the moment.* What they want/need may not be immediately obvious, and in most cases they can't tell you what it is. But figuring it out is the key to changing the behavior.

For example, during my first five minutes as a class-room teacher, a fifteen-year-old boy threw a dictionary at me when my back was turned. Naturally, my first instinct was to send him to the principal's office. But my second thought was, *Why would a boy come to school and throw a book at a teacher when he knows exactly what will happen?* I'll try to explain my thought process from that point. It went something like this: *This boy's behavior makes no sense, unless he is psychotic. He doesn't look psychotic, so I will assume there is some other reason for his behavior.*

Clearly, he expects to be sent to the principal's office. Perhaps he wants to go to the office. Why? He must want out of this room very badly. Why would that be? He doesn't even know me. He must be afraid I will find out something about him. I teach English. Perhaps he has poor grammar skills or hates to write. Perhaps he can't read.

As it turned out, my third guess was right. The boy couldn't read. I taught him how, but first I explained to him privately that I believed he wanted out of my classroom for some reason. I told him if he found me insufferable, he was welcome to go to the counselor and request a different English teacher. But I also told him that I believed he was afraid I would find out something about him, and that's why he had thrown the book at me. I promised him that I would not embarrass or humiliate him in my classroom, that I would provide challenging work but would help him accomplish it, and that I would help him overcome whatever problems he had had in the past in his English classes. He chose to stay in my class, learned to read, and stopped by my room to show me his high school diploma three years later.

Here is another example of a child's behavior that seemed completely irrational to us adults, but made perfectly good sense to the boy involved. Eric was a high school freshman who attended every class, but never participated or completed his assignments. He never disrupted class, but answered all my questions with a shrug. It took a full year of stubborn, silent failure before Eric finally confided that the reason he didn't try in school was because he knew he couldn't earn straight A's—something he believed his mother expected. Since he couldn't bear to disappoint his mother by earning less than perfect grades, he earned nothing. His theory was, If I don't try, I can't fail. When I finally convinced Eric to explain his behavior and later explained the situation to his mother, she was shocked. She had never demanded perfect grades and had tried everything she could think of to encourage and motivate her son.

"Where did he ever get such a crazy idea?" she asked. He wouldn't tell her, but he did tell me. His answer: "I was outside playing one day and I heard my mom talking to my aunt. She said why couldn't I be like my cousin who got all A's in school?"

Nobody wants to be disliked or to be a failure. So when students are failing, or acting in ways that perplex, infuriate, or irritate us, there is a reason. There is a reason for everything children do. Finding that reason is the first step to solving the problem.

I was a "little stinker" when I was in school. I earned high grades, but I did so in the most disruptive way possible. Why did I torment my teachers? Because my older sister was more popular than I was. Because my brothers— and all the boys in town—were allowed much more freedom than I was. Because some of my teachers used shame and humiliation as their primary teaching techniques. Because I was bored with the pace in some of my classes and struggled to keep up in others. My reasons weren't unique and they aren't important now, except that remembering my own misbehavior as a child, and analyzing it from an adult perspective, often provides insight into my own students' behavior.

Other insight comes from my experiences as an enlisted broadcast journalist in the U.S. Navy, as a psychology major in college, as an officer in the U.S. Marine Corps, and as a graduate student of education. This unlikely combination of experiences provides me with a rather unusual perspective of the world, along with a variety of methods and techniques I would not otherwise have at my disposal. At navy boot camp, for example, I learned how frustrating it is to be powerless, and how ineffective punishment can be when it is unreasonable. My psychology professors taught me to understand why people do what they do. At Marine Corps Officer Candidate School I received the best possible training in leadership and a deeply rooted self-confidence. And, although critics of U.S. university teacher training programs would have you believe otherwise, from my graduate studies in education I learned many techniques and theories that directly contribute to my success in the classroom.

I believe that many of those same teaching techniques and theories can be adapted for use by parents. I also believe that many of the most valuable lessons of my life have been taught to me by students. It is my hope that by sharing my philosophies and experiences with you, and the lessons I've learned from my students, together we can make the classroom education of your children less painful and traumatic, and perhaps even *(dare we hope?)* enjoyable.

Subjects included in this book are not presented in order of importance, but in order of my own approach to any given class. I assume that what I need to know to be an effective teacher is the same information that will help you be an effective monitor of your child's education. At first glance, it may seem to you that I spend too much time on background information before we get to the nitty-gritty, but it has been my experience that the time and effort we put into preparation pays off—it not only prevents many problems, but they are much easier to deal with when they do arise (and they will).

Good luck. Being a parent is the most difficult and important job in the world. You already have my respect and admiration. This book is my offer of assistance. If it gives you even one new idea or inspiration (or reassurance that you're "doing it right"), I will consider this effort a resounding success. By the way, any comments or criticisms you may have, or any sharing of your own experiences, would be most welcome. Please write to me in care of my publisher (and please be patient—I will respond).

P.S. In the first paragraph of this chapter, I stated that I have no children of my own, but I recently married the love of my life who came complete with four lovely children, ages six to fourteen. My stepchildren have graciously, although unknowingly, tested the theories and practices in this book and proved them feasible. So far, so good.

Chapter 2

MEET THE TEACHER

✼

W hen I see a parent or guardian accompany a student to Open House, then I know that student is going to pass my class whether or not the kid is smart," a teacher confided as we stood in the hallway outside our classrooms, waiting for the parents to arrive on visitors' night. That was my first Open House, and it was the first time I'd heard a teacher make that remark, but in the following years, I heard it many times. I've said it myself, and I believe it's true. It doesn't matter whether you dropped out of high school or graduated with the highest grades in your class. What matters is that your child believes that you think school is important. *The single most important element that contributes to a child's success in school is having at least one adult at home who believes that education is important and who takes action to demonstrate that belief.*

CHILDREN BELIEVE WHAT THEY SEE, NOT WHAT WE SAY

It isn't enough to simply tell your children that school is important; you need to show them. Children learn far more from what we do than from what we say. Adults are the same. We don't always believe what we hear, but we almost always believe what we see. If you show by your actions that you believe education is important, your children will believe it is. The easiest way to make school important to your child is to visit his or her school. Meet the teachers. Visiting school may seem like a small thing, but it can have a big impact on your child's attitude and success. I could give you hundreds of examples, but I will give you two: Ivan Barela and Joanie Farrington.

Ivan was a student in my freshman English class, a quiet, well-mannered young man who had excellent reading, writing, and spelling skills. Most of the boys in Ivan's class were rowdy, ill-mannered "gangster wannabes" who earned barely passing grades. Ivan could talk as tough as anybody, and he was popular with his classmates, but he never participated in their paper-throwing contests or planned disruptions of my lessons. He wasn't a "brown-nose." Sometimes, he laughed at the other boys' pranks, but if he noticed me looking at him, he would blush and whisper, "Sorry, Miss."

On Parents' Night at our school, I realized why Ivan was so polite and such a good student. He and his grandfather were the first visitors to my room. Mr. Barela was quite elderly and walked with the aid of a cane. Ivan held his grandfather's arm and escorted him to a seat at one of the student desks. I introduced myself and extended my hand to Mr. Barela, who took it between both of his own and said, "*Lo siento. No puedo hablar inglés bien. Pero mucho gusto conocer la maestra de mi hijo.*" (I'm sorry I don't speak English well. But it is a pleasure to meet the teacher of my grandson.) Even though he couldn't speak English, Mr. Barela came to meet Ivan's teachers. Ivan and I both got the message. It didn't matter whether his grandfather was educated, or whether he could speak English. Mr. Barela cared about Ivan and his success in school. Because his grandfather clearly cared so much, Ivan also cared.

JOANIE JUST DOESN'T TAKE HER STUDIES SERIOUSLY

I had another intelligent, well-behaved student, a girl whose parents were both college graduates. I had spoken to Joanie's mother on the phone twice: once when Joanie transferred into my class, and again when she had a D− at the end of the first quarter. Joanie's reading and writing skills were excellent, and I believed she could earn an A if she wanted to. Clearly, she didn't want a good grade. She never turned in her homework, although whenever I asked for her assignments, she always found them tucked inside her textbook. Time and again, she promised to work harder and stop forgetting to hand in her work. She didn't do either. When I requested a conference, Mrs. Farrington said that she and her husband didn't really have time to come to a conference, and they didn't think a conference was necessary. She said they would talk to Joanie, and she was sure that would be the end of the problem because Joanie had always been such a good girl.

Joanie's grade improved slightly, and she was carrying a D+ when the night for Open House arrived. I sent a personal invitation to Mr. and Mrs. Farrington. Joanie reported that she thought they would both come, but neither of them did. Joanie came by herself and spent the evening walking around with the family of one of her classmates. As the family left my classroom, I asked Joanie to stay behind for a minute.

"I'm sorry I didn't get to meet your parents," I said.

"They were going to come," Joanie said. "But my mom had to work and my dad had a meeting to go to. So they asked Sharon's mom if I could come with them instead."

The following day, I called Mr. Farrington at work and told him I thought perhaps Joanie was trying to get their attention by earning poor grades in school.

"That's silly," Mr. Farrington said. "Joanie is very intelligent. She just doesn't take her studies seriously. But when she gets out of school and can't find a job, she'll wake up." I was tempted to tell Mr. Farrington that perhaps he was the one who needed to wake up, but he didn't have time to talk; he had an important call waiting on the other line.

FOR EVERY EXCUSE, THERE IS AN ARGUMENT

Why don't parents and guardians go to Open House at school? There are a lot of reasons: Too busy, too tired, too whatever. They may be perfectly good reasons, and valid ones, but they are not good excuses. As a teacher, I've heard some of the most creative, inventive excuses in the world. Here are the most common reasons parents give for not visiting school, and my arguments against them.

Reason 1: I'm Just Too Busy with Work/Little Children/ Sick Parents.   If there is no way you can leave work or home, then find somebody else to go—but send *somebody*. If your child has an older brother or sister, a cousin, an aunt or uncle, or a grandparent, ask one of them to go in your place. If no family member is available, ask a neighbor. Don't worry that a teacher will be reluctant to talk to a sixteen-year-old or an adult who isn't related to the student. Most teachers would welcome anybody who cares about a child enough to visit school and find out how the child is doing. Actually, you may be doing a favor by asking somebody to visit school for you. People enjoy helping children, and it makes them feel good about themselves to know that they have contributed to the success of a child. My parents visited my school and paid close attention to my report card, but after my parents signed my card, I always took it next door to show my neighbor, Edys. Edys's children were grown and gone off on their own, and she missed them. Edys would sit down and inspect my report card carefully. She'd ask me why I earned each mark, then she'd hug me and give me a homemade cookie. At the time, I thought I was the one who was "getting the goods." Looking back, I realize that Edys enjoyed the report card ritual as much as I did.

Reason 2: I Work Hard at a Full-Time Job. I'm Just Too Tired to Go. Anybody who can hold down a full-time job and raise children at the same time earns my respect and admiration. It isn't easy, I know. And I can certainly understand the meaning of the word *tired*. But I honestly believe that it's worth being exhausted for a while to visit your children's school. You may miss a few hours of rest, but you will know immediately if your child is having problems in school and will be able to take some corrective action. *Or* you may find out that your hard work has paid off and your child is doing well—which should help you get a good night's sleep.

If you don't visit the school because you're too tired, imagine how much more tired you will feel when you have to pick up your disruptive child at the principal's office or you have to sign a report card filled with failing grades. And, in the worst case, imagine how you'll feel when your child drops out of school or flunks out or can't find a job, or when you end up sitting in the visitor's room of the courthouse, waiting to talk to a police officer about your truant or delinquent child. It may seem as though I'm exaggerating, but I am not. Children who succeed in school tend to succeed in life, but the odds are stacked against children who fail in school. The sooner you become aware of any problems at school, the better chance you have of getting your child back on track.

Reason 3: Teachers Make Me Uncomfortable. They're So Critical. Maybe you are reluctant to visit your child's school because your own school years were miserable. Maybe you can't spell, and spent twelve miserable years listening to people complain about it. Maybe you're ashamed of your imperfect grammar. Or perhaps your family budget doesn't include fashionable clothing, and you are afraid that the teacher will look down on you or that your children will be embarrassed for their friends to see you.

First, you need to remember something important—intelligence and education are two very different things. You can be very intelligent without having any education. And you can be very well-educated without being intelligent. We all know smart people who act stupid. Good grammar doesn't necessarily mean big brains. So, don't worry that the teacher is going to criticize your language skills or think less of you because your grammar isn't perfect. (If she does, she is far more ignorant than you could ever be.)

As far as clothing is concerned, schoolteachers are never featured on *Lifestyles of the Rich and Famous*; they know what it means to live on a budget. Teachers are not in a position to criticize other people's wardrobes. Ask your children. I'm sure they can tell you about a teacher who wears the same jacket or dress every single Monday. If you wear a uniform to work and that's all you have, then wear your uniform to school, even if it has grease or dirt on it.

No matter what you wear, your kids may complain that your fashion statement is an embarrassment to them.

Don't listen to them. Kids enjoy complaining about their parents. In fact, for many teenagers, that is one of their favorite hobbies. I remember being ashamed of my parents when I was in seventh grade, my first year at Youngsville (Pennsylvania) Junior-Senior High School. I didn't want to be seen in public with my mother, who wore white ankle socks and black oxford shoes with her dresses (which were never the latest style), or my father, who worked as a welder and wore a navy blue shirt and trousers and heavy leather boots. "Please don't humiliate me like this. Let me stay home," I begged as my family crowded into our station wagon for the Open House. But they made me go, along with my four brothers and sisters.

When my parents entered one of my teachers' classrooms, I walked slowly, hoping that if I put enough distance between us, people might think they belonged to some other unlucky twelve-year-old. I tried to pretend I didn't know my father when he shook each teacher's hand and said, "I'm LouAnne's father, Bob Johnson, and this here is my wife, Shirley. If you ever have any problems with our daughter, you just let me know and I'll make sure it don't happen again." None of my teachers laughed. In fact, they seemed to like my parents, in spite of their weird clothing and working-class language. And I have to admit that I was secretly pleased that my parents took the time to visit every teacher every year, although I would have lied my face off if anybody had accused me of enjoying those visits at the time.

Reason 4: Why Bother? They're Just Going to Blame Me for What's Wrong.   Maybe you've done your best to be a good parent, to teach your children right from wrong, and they still act terribly in school. You don't want to hear the same list of complaints from teachers, and you're tired of being blamed for everything your child does.

Why bother? Because the teacher needs to know that you have tried to set a good example. If you are doing your job, providing the best role model you can for your child, and he or she still has problems in school, it's very important for you to tell the teacher. If your child isn't following *your* example, then he or she is following *somebody else's* example—most likely another student, an unsuccessful student. If you and the teacher can determine who is influencing your child, you may be able to figure out a strategy for limiting that person's influence. But if you don't let the teacher know that you care about your child's education, the teacher may assume that you don't.

Please don't take a teacher's remarks about your child's behavior as criticism of you as a person or as a parent. We all know that children are strongly influenced by their friends and other people, such as athletes, television and movie stars, and singers. Any intelligent teacher will understand that your child may behave terribly at school, although you have tried to teach her good manners. The important thing isn't to find somebody to blame for your child's misbehavior, but to work together to change the behavior.

Last year, one of the boys in my seventh period freshman English class, Michael Barr, starting cutting class during the last quarter of the school year. His grade dropped quickly from a B to a D, and I asked the guidance counselor for advice. The counselor said he had called Michael's mother and learned that she knew Michael was leaving school early. Mrs. Barr had already taken away

Michael's telephone and television privileges, but he still kept cutting. She wasn't sure what to do next because the boy who was picking up Michael from school was her employer's son, Jeff, an unemployed high school graduate. She had talked to her boss about the problem, but was afraid if she pressed the issue, her boss would become defensive and she'd lose her job.

I stopped Michael in the hallway and asked him why he was cutting my class. He didn't lie. He said he was leaving every day with a friend who picked him up. He said he didn't want to cut, but just couldn't say no. I told Michael that I understood how tempting it must be to cut and asked if he would like some help. He said he would. I told the principal about Michael's problem, and he asked if I could find out the color and make of Jeff's car. It wasn't difficult—Michael told me. The principal then alerted our security officer to stop the car and ask Jeff why he was coming on campus every day. Since he had no legitimate excuse, Jeff was not permitted to park on campus. Michael stopped cutting class and his grades improved. If Michael's mother hadn't explained her situation, we might have assumed that she simply didn't care.

If you have a problem, try talking to a teacher. Yes, I realize that you may run into a teacher who doesn't care, but chances are good that you'll find one who does.

Reason 5: Teachers Need to Do Their Jobs. They Get Paid to Teach.   Sometimes teachers complain, "I'm supposed to be the teacher, not the parent." And indignant parents claim, "It's the teacher's job to teach my child, not mine." I disagree with both of those positions. I think it is the job of both parent and teacher to make sure children learn academic skills and how to behave as decent people. We share different aspects of the same job, and if we work together, we have a much better chance of success.

If you do encounter a teacher who seems more interested in blaming you than in solving your child's problems, then you might want to consider requesting a different teacher. However, requesting a transfer is a serious matter and something that should be done only as a last resort. (I'll talk more about this later on.)

Reason 6: I'm Shy. I Never Know What to Say.   You don't have to do all the talking. All you need to do is say, "Hello, I am So-and-So's father/mother/aunt/grandfather/guardian. I'm very happy to meet you. And I would like to know how So-and-So is doing in your class." The teacher will take it from there. You may have three or four children in school, but most full-time teachers have over 150 students! They have a lot of practice talking to parents and guardians and should be prepared to discuss your child's progress in detail.

Reason 7: We Don't Speak English Very Well.   What if your family doesn't speak English? (Don't laugh! I realize that a non-English speaker isn't likely to be reading this paragraph—but that doesn't mean friends and relatives won't. If you know a non–English-speaking adult, why not offer your help?)

Write a note telling the teacher about the language barrier. Even a non–English-speaking adult can be shown a student's papers or other projects and will be able to tell a lot from the teacher's tone of voice and facial expressions.

If possible, bring your child along to act as interpreter. Children love to translate; it makes them feel important. It is an advantage in today's society to speak more than one language, so I encourage students to take every opportunity to use their bilingual speaking skills. When it's time for your child to apply for jobs, the ability to speak multiple languages will be a major asset. Many businesspeople pay thousands of dollars to learn a second language. A bilingual student enters the business world one step and more than a few dollars ahead.

DON'T WORRY—BE HAPPY

Go to school. Meet the teachers. Don't worry. You won't get a report card for going to Open House—but if you did, you would earn an A for effort. Caring about your children will earn you a high grade in any good teacher's book.

A MEETING OF THE MINDS

Sometimes there is a time limit for visits during Open House. Sometimes they are meant as a "handshake and a smile night," with no time allowed for conversations about individual students. If that is the case, ask the teacher when you could schedule a conference or when would be the best time to call to arrange a meeting. If you can't contact the teacher by phone (some schools have no outside lines for teachers to use), send a note to school with your child, giving your home telephone number and asking the teacher to call you. If that doesn't work, contact the guidance office or the principal's administrative assistant and ask to schedule a meeting. If you arrange a conference via the office with a teacher you haven't met, the teacher might assume that you have a complaint about his or her teaching, so it's a good idea to explain that you want to discuss your child's progress in class and find out what you can do to help your child be successful. (Even if you suspect that the teacher is the primary problem, your purpose should still be to find out what you can do to help your child.)

At the conference, your first comments will set the tone for the meeting. That's why I don't think it's wise to complain about your child until you find out what the teacher thinks. Many times I've been surprised to hear a parent say that a child has a learning disability or a behavior problem or a bad attitude, because that student had been doing very well in my class. Teachers' expectations for students are very important. Numerous studies show the same result: Students succeed when teachers expect them to succeed; they fail when teachers expect them to fail. So, you might not want to begin by telling the teacher that you have a problem child. Instead, wait and see whether the teacher thinks your child has a problem. If the teacher compliments your child, then maybe you need to change your own expectations. Parents' expectations affect children as much as teachers' expectations do. If you expect them to misbehave, why should they behave?

BE PREPARED TO ASK QUESTIONS

Maybe you are willing to schedule a conference but aren't sure what to ask the teacher. Here is a list of questions to get you started:

1. What are the requirements for this class or course?
2. How is my child doing? Is she/he at the top, middle, or bottom of the class?
3. What can I do to help my child learn the information or skills for this class?
4. Is there any particular problem area that you have noticed?
5. Is my child quiet, talkative, well-behaved, or disruptive in class?
6. Does my child have a particular friend or friends in this classroom?
7. Are those friends good students or are they disruptive?
8. Where does my child sit in this classroom? (If the child needs glasses or a hearing aid, be sure the teacher knows—some kids hide them.)
9. Could I see essays or reports that my child has written? Exam papers? Artwork or projects?
10. If you think my child needs special help, where can I find it?

BE AVAILABLE

Sometimes kids count on the fact that teachers and parents don't have much chance to communicate. They become expert at playing them against each other. The simplest way to avoid this situation is to talk to every teacher. If you have an irregular work schedule or must travel frequently, let the teachers know. Give them your home or work phone number and the best times to call. If you can't be disturbed at work, make sure teachers know. (If there is a nonmedical emergency, such as a fight, who should they call?)

If your child makes a habit of cutting classes, you might want to call the school periodically and check to see if your child is present in class. As I said earlier, few teachers have outside telephone lines in their classrooms, so you may not be able to call the teacher directly. But you can call the office and ask that a message be delivered to the teacher immediately. Most offices have student clerks or runners who will either call or walk to the classroom at your request and find out whether your child is present in class. Don't worry about causing extra work—I don't know a single administrator or teacher who would complain about a parent who is trying to improve poor student attendance. Even if they do complain, don't listen. A grumpy attendance clerk is better than a truant child.

SHOPPING 101

In my classroom at one high school, I was fortunate to have a telephone that could receive direct incoming calls. During that year, one of my sophomore girls began skipping class during second period, taking a bus to a nearby shopping center, and taking another bus back during lunch. When Deanne's mother and I found out, we devised a plan. At the start of every third period, Deanne's mother called my room. If Deanne was absent, her mother met her at the door when she got home from school and handed her a list of extra chores to complete before dinner. After a couple of weeks, Deanne stopped cutting second and third periods, but then she started cutting her afternoon classes!

With the help of another teacher, Deanne's mother and I came up with a new plan. Whenever Deanne was absent, the teacher called me, I called Deanne's mother, and she took off work and came directly to school. When Deanne stepped off the bus, Mother was right there waiting for her. The third time that happened, her mother announced that if Deanne didn't stop cutting, she had two choices: Her mother would take a temporary leave from her job and escort Deanne to every single class, sitting in the back of the room during the entire class period, or she would disenroll Deanne, quit her day job, and sign up for home schooling. She also pointed out that they would not be eating any take-out food or renting any videos for the next few weeks because her paycheck would be smaller owing to the time she had taken off from work because of Deanne's cutting. Furthermore, if she had to quit her day job and work during the evenings, their budget would be even smaller.

"My mom loves her job," Deanne told me. "Do you really think she'd quit and home-school me?"

"What do you think?" I countered. Deanne thought for a minute, then nodded.

"Yeah, I think she'd quit. And I think she'd make me real sorry, too."

"Maybe she would," I said, "but she wouldn't quit her job if she didn't love you so much, would she?"

Deanne's eyebrows shot up. That thought hadn't occurred to her. Apparently, it finally sank in. She quit cutting classes and her grades improved.

THE DESPERATE DAD

Another student, Kris Witherspoon, cut school so often that he was classified as a truant. Kris was an honors student and a talented musician who sometimes earned money playing his trumpet. He didn't think he needed a high school diploma. Kris's father tried many tactics, including coming to school every day during his lunch break to check on Kris. Unlike Deanne, Kris didn't try to sneak out of school; he stopped coming completely.

Eventually, Mr. Witherspoon ran out of time and patience. He went to the administration office and officially disenrolled his son from school. A few days later, when Kris decided to show up at school for a few hours, he was informed that he was no longer a student on our rolls. Kris was flabbergasted. When he protested, Mr. Witherspoon said, "You're sixteen years old, and you insist that you're old enough to make your own decisions. Fine. But that means you are also old enough to support yourself. Since you don't want to go to school, your mother and I expect you to find a job and pay room and board while you live with us. We love you, but we can't be responsible for you if you refuse to be responsible for yourself." Kris stormed out of the house (a very large and comfortable house, by the way) and vowed never to return. Two weeks later, he was back. When I told him I was happy to see him back in school, he shrugged and said, "I might as well stay. I'm not old enough to work in the clubs full time, and you can't get a decent job if you don't have a diploma."

The things these parents did may sound extreme, but sometimes that's what it takes. When Deanne's mother was willing to jeopardize her job, Deanne finally believed that her mother cared about her. And when Kris realized that his parents would not permit him to act immature and take advantage of them, he decided to grow up.

Maybe neither of those solutions would have worked with a different child. Working with children is never easy. Every time we solve one problem, they come up with another one. When I feel overwhelmed, I rely on my sense of humor to help me persevere. I remind myself that it is children's job to drive us crazy, and they're very good at their work. I only hope that they'll be as talented and resourceful in their future careers.

ARRANGE FOR REGULAR FEEDBACK

It is important to stay in contact with your children's teachers via progress reports, phone calls, or regular conferences. Knowing that parents and teachers talk to each other regularly is a powerful incentive for students to behave. But phone calls aren't enough for some students; they need more incentive to attend classes, behave themselves, and keep their grades up. Many parents of my students use regular weekly progress reports. Sometimes, printed report forms are available from the guidance or administration office. If not, you can make your own (see sample Progress Report form on page 30). If you have access to a typewriter or word processor, fine. If not, just print your form on a piece of paper and make copies so you will have a good supply. Forty-five copies should be enough to provide a weekly report for the entire school year, unless your child has year-round school.

Some parents simply want to know that the student was in class. Others want to know whether homework was completed, or whether a certain behavior has occurred (talking too much, fighting with others, homework turned in, etc.). Try to keep your form short and easy to complete, so the teacher can quickly check the appropriate sections before or after class.

MAKE SURE YOU GET THE REAL REPORT

Now, of course, I know that *your* child would never fib to you, so you won't need to read this next part—it's for those parents whose children are sometimes less than truthful. Believe it or not, I have had students who fill out their own progress reports and forge their teachers' signatures! (Can you imagine? I'm sure *you* never forged your parents' signatures or tried to sneak your way out of trouble.) I have also had students who go through the mail before their parents get home from work and remove any envelopes that have the school's return address.

Still, I would suggest giving your child one chance to be honest before you get sneaky yourself. Send your progress report to school with your child on Monday and make it clear that you expect to have the report back in your hands immediately after school on Friday. If your child says the report was lost, he or she might be telling the truth, but it might have been lost on purpose—or not filled out at all. If your child comes home without the report, please don't ask the teachers to fill out two the following week, one for the current week and one for the previous week (many teachers have to turn in their attendance sheets to the office every Friday). Instead, switch to an alternative method. You could drop off the report at the guidance office on Monday morning, ask your child's guidance counselor to make sure it is delivered to the teacher(s), and pick it up yourself from the counselor on Friday afternoon. Or provide a self-addressed stamped envelope for the report to be mailed to you when it is filled out by the last teacher on the form (use a plain envelope and address it by hand so your child won't know the report is inside). I once sent notices to parents of absent students on bright pink paper. One boy burst into my classroom a few days later and pointed his finger at me.

"That was pretty sneaky of you, Miss J, sending my mom a note on pink paper and writing that sloppy address on the outside. I went through the mail, but I didn't open that letter because it didn't look official."

"I know," I said, "but I know your mom cares about you and she would want to know that you were absent from my class. If we didn't love you, we wouldn't care what you did, would we?"

The next time I sent a note to his mother, I typed the

address on the envelope and included a return address from a fictional company. If you are allowed to receive personal mail at your business or workplace, you might ask your child's teacher to send mail to you at work.

IF YOUR LITTLE DARLING PROTESTS

Some students become very angry when their parents arrange for regular progress reports. "You don't trust me!" they accuse. My response would be, "When you bring home a report card with all passing grades, and your attendance shows no unexcused absences, I will stop asking for progress reports. Until then, I am trying to help you learn to be more responsible. That's my job as your parent."

Your child may try to doctor the progress report, so you won't learn about those absences or low grades. If that happens, try to remember that kids don't do these things because they are bad—they do them because they are afraid or immature. Can you remember when you got in trouble in school and you were afraid your parents were "going to kill you" when they found out? I surely can. If you catch them trying to cover up grades, then ask why they feel a need to hide the truth. Is it because they are afraid you won't like them anymore? Are they afraid you will hit them or punish them in some other way? If so, reconsider. Punishing children for doing poorly in school isn't a very effective way to encourage them to change. Punishment makes them angry, but it doesn't usually change their behavior. Think of how you would react if your boss wrote a report on your performance every week. What would encourage you to do better if you were performing poorly? Losing your paycheck, or getting some special help or training? Would you rather hear a lecture, or participate in a conversation with your boss to find out exactly what is expected of you?

A child's job is to go to school. If you catch your child lying to prevent you from learning about his misbehavior or poor grades, make it clear that you will not tolerate dishonesty because you are trying to help him. Establish the rules and explain exactly what will happen if he lies again. What should those consequences be? It's up to you to decide what would be most effective for your child, but here are some things that have worked with my students:

- a conference with the teacher, parent, and student
- a written apology from the child to the teacher(s) involved
- extra work after school—cleaning the classroom, picking up trash, etc.
- meeting with the parent, student, and principal
- sign up the student for regular tutoring before, during, or after school
- permission to play sports only if grades and/or behavior remain good
- require the student to attend summer school to improve poor grade(s)
- require daily study sessions at home, with parental supervision
- extra chores at home or loss of TV, phone, or social privileges

I think it's important to include some kind of reward when the student's attendance, behavior, and/or grades improve. Wouldn't you be more enthusiastic about improving your performance at work if your boss gave you a promotion, a bonus, a raise, or some other recognition?

Okay, before I forget, here are my sample reports (see pages 30 and 31). The first one is for an elementary school student who has only one teacher; the second is for secondary students who have several teachers.

SHOULD YOUR CONFERENCE BE PRIVATE?

Some experts recommend including students in any parent-teacher conference; others believe it's better to meet without the student. I think it depends upon your relationship with your child, the child's relationship with the teacher, and the reason for the conference. If you think a confidential teacher-parent conference is necessary, then I would urge you to keep it truly private—don't tell your child. If she finds out, be honest and say that you wanted to learn what you could do to help her succeed in school, but didn't want to make her nervous or anxious about the meeting.

I think the best plan is to include the student in the parent-teacher conference, for at least part of the meeting. If children think we are "ganging up on them," they will often become more stubborn and resistant to changing their behavior. If they attend the conference, they won't be as likely to think we are talking behind their backs. If your child does attend a conference, try to include her in

Sample Progress Report for student with only one teacher.

PROGRESS REPORT for the week beginning _____

Student's name _____ Home telephone: _____

Teacher's name _____ Room No. _____

	Monday	Tuesday	Wednesday	Thursday	Friday
Present in class (please mark T if tardy)					
Homework turned in	Yes/No	Yes/No	Yes/No	Yes/No	Yes/No
Behavior acceptable	Yes/No	Yes/No	Yes/No	Yes/No	Yes/No

Is student passing your class at present time?   Yes   No   _____
                                                              Teacher's signature

Sample Progress Report for students with more than one teacher.

PROGRESS REPORT for the week beginning _____

Student Name: _____

Teachers: Please mark **Yes** or **No** for each day to indicate student's presence and completed work. If no homework was assigned, print N/A. Please use <u>ink</u>. Thank you.

	Mon present/homework	Tues present/homework	Wed present/homework	Thur present/homework	Fri present/homework	Teacher signature
Period 1						
Period 2						
Period 3						
Period 4						
Period 5						
Period 6						
Period 7						

If student's present grade is presently D or below, please circle class period: 1   2   3   4   5   6   7

Comments: _____

the conversation—it's insulting when people talk about you as though you weren't in the room.

My recommendation is to include your child at the beginning of the conference, then excuse her while you talk to the teacher privately. Then, call your child back into the meeting and explain whatever strategy you and the teacher have agreed upon. Depending upon your child's maturity and attitude, you might want to ask for her opinion about your plan. But I wouldn't allow the child to veto the plan. I think it's important for children to see parents and teachers working together as a team, but I also think it's important for children to understand that it is the adults who have the responsibility of making decisions for them until they demonstrate that they are able to make them for themselves. Somebody has to be the "bad guy"—and I would rather it be me or you than your child.

Chapter 3

MONITOR THAT
HOMEWORK

✣

SEEING IS BELIEVING

Even the most conscientious, intelligent parent can be fooled by a creative homework alibi. When Dad asks to see Shawna's homework before she goes out to play softball, Shawna shows him a worksheet she did last semester. When Jeremy wants to play video games after school and Mom says homework comes first, Jeremy crosses his heart and hopes to spit that he worked really really hard and finished his work at school. Shawna plays ball, Jeremy eliminates evil space creatures, and Mom and Dad are satisfied that they've done their duty. Everybody is happy—until the report cards arrive.

ASK THE TEACHER

Kids don't lie about homework because they are immoral, unethical scoundrels. They lie for the same reason adults do: They think if they ignore something long enough, it will go away. Or because they'd rather have fun than work. Or because they are tired of thinking all day. Or because they honestly forgot all about it. That's why I recommend talking to your children's teachers. Most teachers have a standard policy about homework. Many elementary teachers assign homework every weekday, to get children into the habit of working at home. Some secondary teachers, especially math teachers, also assign daily homework. But sometimes teachers assign homework only as necessary. If you don't have time to visit the school, call each teacher or mail a short note asking them to let you know how often they assign homework. You might also want to ask that the teachers please notify you if your child misses any assignments. It's also a good idea to check with the teacher periodically (I would recommend once a month) to ask whether your child is keeping up with his or her schoolwork. By the time grades are issued, even interim grades, it is sometimes too late to complete enough work to raise a poor or failing grade.

MAKE SURE IT'S THE REAL THING

When you ask to see your child's homework, don't just accept any old paper. Look at it. Make sure it isn't some old paper that has already been graded. Check to see that it contains information that matches the subject—for example, a list of spelling words probably wasn't assigned as math homework. Be prepared: Younger children are usually delighted to show off their work, but older children may complain. They may accuse you of not trusting them or treating them like babies. If that happens, explain that it isn't a matter of trust or maturity. It's a matter of taking your responsibility as a parent or guardian seriously. You might even compare your responsibility at home to your boss's responsibility at work. Your supervisor monitors your work and offers advice when you're having problems because it is his or her responsibility to make sure your work meets company standards. Likewise, you monitor your children's homework because it's your job to make sure your children are well-educated.

Note: Teenagers may complain even after you've offered this brilliant explanation, but don't pay any attention to them. Secretly, they will be pleased that you care enough about them to check their homework, but it's *their* job to complain.

CAN'T HANDLE CALCULUS? DON'T WORRY

What if your children are taking advanced courses that are over your head? Don't be intimidated. I wouldn't know a cosine from a cucumber, but I could tell whether my child was doing her calculus homework. I could still insist that she get after-school tutoring or spend more time on homework if her grades are poor and she seems to be having trouble with the work.

DON'T BE THE LONE RANGER

If your child needs help with his homework and you can't do it, don't be afraid to ask for help. The guidance counselors at your child's school may be able to direct you to a tutoring program. If not, try your local library. If there is a college nearby, the education department may already have a tutoring program in place. If not, they may be able to recommend a student helper. Another option would be to find a high school or college student in your neighborhood and hire him or her as a tutor. There is another source that many people overlook—retired people. Why not put a notice on the bulletin board at your local senior citizens' center asking for a tutor?

STARING ISN'T STUDYING

I once had a freshman class in which half of the students failed most of the spelling and vocabulary exams. These were bright students. They did well on their in-school assignments and most of them did their homework regularly. But they didn't do well on tests. One day, after a particularly pathetic showing on an exam, I put my hands on my hips and stared at my class. "Don't you lie to me, you little stinkers," I said. "I want the truth. How many of you honestly studied for more than fifteen minutes for this test?" Nearly every student raised his or her hand.

"How could you get these grades if you studied?" I asked. Lila Jordan, who sat in the front row, took my criticism to heart.

"I'm not lying, Miss J," Lila cried. "I studied really really hard. Honest." Several other kids echoed her. They, too, had studied really really really hard.

"Oh, you did, did you?" I said. "Well, how did you study? Show me." Lila and her classmates frowned at me, puzzled by my request. "I want to see *how* you studied," I explained. "Show me exactly what you did."

Lila picked up her spelling list and held it in front of her face. "I studied like this," she said, staring at the paper. "Me, too," said a chorus of voices.

"But what are you doing?" I asked Lila.

"I'm studying the words," she said, still staring at the paper.

"Are you spelling them out in your mind?" I asked. She shook her head. No.

"Are you closing your eyes while you spell a word, then opening your eyes to check whether you got it right?" No. She wasn't doing that either.

"Then what are you doing?" I asked.

"I'm not doing anything," Lila said. "I'm just studying."

From the expressions on the faces of the other students, I knew most of them had been "studying" the same way Lila did. They thought that studying meant staring at a piece of paper or a book, as though the information would be magically transferred from the pages to their brains!

I felt terrible. I had been yelling at those students, criticizing them for not trying hard enough, for being too lazy to study, when that wasn't the case at all. They had been trying; they just didn't know how to study. Nobody had ever taught them, or they hadn't learned the lesson. After more discussion, it turned out that a few kids did have good study skills, and they eagerly shared their techniques with their classmates. One boy demonstrated his method for studying spelling. He read the words out loud, singing them to his own little tune. When he could say them all, he practiced writing them down, checking and rechecking until he could spell them all. His method for vocabulary: He numbered one to twenty and wrote the words down the left side of a piece of paper with a brief definition following each word. Then, he took a clean piece of paper and placed it over the definitions, so he could read only the words. He would go down the list and write down the definition for each word. When he finished, he simply had to compare his answer sheet to the original paper to see which words he needed to study.

One girl, an only child, explained how she gave herself her own practice spelling test when her parents weren't available to read the words out to her. She wrote down a brief definition of each spelling word on a large piece of paper (for example, she used "not allow" to remind her of the spelling word "prohibit" and "something you must have" as the prompt for "necessary"). She would tape the paper with the definitions up in front of her desk and try to write the correct spellings of the words on the exam list. One of her friends suggested it would be easier to simply read the word list into a tape recorder and use that as a prompt to do her practice exams.

Another girl said she taped her spelling list up on the bathroom mirror where she could look at it while she brushed her teeth every morning and night. "After I look at those words for a couple of days," she said, "it's like they are printed in my brain and I can see them in my mind when we have a test." To make sure she remembered, she also did "air writing"—using her finger as an imaginary pencil to write the words in the air. This technique, as I learned later, is especially helpful for kinesthetic students, those who learn by doing or movement better than they do by sight or sound. (I'll talk more about learning styles in a later chapter.)

After school that day, I stopped a the guidance office and asked the counselors if they could recommend a book for teaching basic study skills. They referred me to the school librarian, who showed me a book and a couple of pamphlets. She also suggested that I check the reference section at the public library and the local bookstore. I checked out several books and took notes from the ones I thought had the best tips. Then I took my notes to class and tried to help my students learn how to learn. Yes, I know, they should already have learned those basic skills by the time they were in high school, but they hadn't learned them, and I think it's more important to help children succeed than it is to find somebody to blame for their failure.

Many study skills books are short, less than 100 pages, and contain simple, specific instructions that any adult can use to help children learn to study effectively. I won't go into details here, because teaching a second grader how to study is very different from teaching a high school sophomore. Younger children are asked to used memorization skills quite frequently, for example, whereas older students should be using higher level skills such as analysis and evaluation. But I do recommend reading some of the how-to-study books available in your community. If you have trouble finding something suitable, ask your school guidance counselor or librarian for help. Or ask your school librarian for the names of some textbook publishers and call to ask them if they publish study guides.

THE SOUND OF MUSIC

If your child knows how to study, but still has trouble concentrating on homework, there could be a number of reasons. Your house may be too noisy—or too quiet. Believe it or not, some kids learn better in a noisy environment, perhaps because they have to concentrate to drown out the noise. If your son insists that he studies better while wearing a blaring stereo headset, he may be telling' the truth. I've tried letting students wear headphones in my classroom during exams—and their improved grades convinced me to let them listen to music as long as it didn't distract other students. (I know it's against the rules at many schools, but I'd rather take my chances if it means better learning for my students. The kids hide their headsets if somebody comes into the room. Occasionally, we get caught. Then I take full responsibility for breaking the rule. I apologize profusely and promise to be a good girl in the future. I know some people might think I'm setting a bad example, and maybe I am, but I'm also teaching children to question unreasonable rules. I honestly don't understand why people would rather have children earn poor grades than let them listen to music if it helps them.)

If your children want to listen to music while studying, why not conduct your own experiment? Let them listen to music at their chosen volume for as long as their grades are good. If their grades go down, so does the volume of the music. You might be surprised at the results.

SHEDDING SOME LIGHT ON THE SUBJECT

Another obstacle to effective studying may be the light in your home. I'm not talking about light being too soft— sometimes bright light is the culprit.

"How many times have I told you not to read in the dark?" my mother always asked when she caught me reading by flashlight under my covers after I was supposed to be asleep. My mother believed, as many people do, that bright light is best for reading, but recent studies indicate that dim light may actually be better for some readers whose eyes are more sensitive to light levels.

In recent years, the issue of scotopic sensitivity has aroused considerable interest—and inspired many arguments. In simplest terms, scotopic sensitivity (light sensitivity) concerns the eye's ability to filter different colors from the spectrum of light. It means that different people's eyes respond differently to various intensities and sources of light (sunlight, fluorescent lights, incandescent bulbs, etc.). Some people have trouble reading under fluorescent lighting or from pages that are glossy, for example. Some people prefer very bright, direct light for reading while others need indirect, soft lighting.

Light sensitivity is not a vision problem, such as nearsightedness. In fact, most people who perform tests for scotopic sensitivity require an eye exam prior to light sensitivity testing to make sure that it is not a vision problem that is causing a person's discomfort or difficulty when reading.

Some people swear that there is a dramatic difference in their ability to read when they change the light source, wear eyeglasses with colored filters in the lenses, or place pastel transparencies over a page of black-and-white print. Other people insist that the whole idea of scotopic sensitivity is so much stuff and nonsense. I'm neither a scientist nor an expert in human vision, so my own opinion about the validity of scotopic sensitivity testing is based on my experiences in the classroom. I am sharing those experiences with you because I believe that we should consider every possible factor that might affect our children's ability to read and learn.

READING MAKES MY EYES CRY

In California, I had a tenth-grade student, Nick, who was very well-behaved in class, except when it came time for individual silent reading. During class sessions when we read out loud, he was fine, but when I insisted that he read by himself, he became so disruptive that I threatened to banish him from my classroom if he didn't settle down. One day, after my threat, he sat down and read for ten minutes, then got up and walked to my desk. "Look," he said. "This happens every time I read. It makes my eyes cry." His eyes—which had looked perfectly normal a few minutes earlier—were bright red and so watery that tears were running down his cheeks.

"How long has this been happening?" I wanted to know. He shrugged.

"As long as I can remember. Whenever I read, I get a really bad headache and my eyes hurt and then they start crying all by themselves."

After class, I called his mother to see whether Nick had medical insurance that covered vision. She said he did and immediately arranged a visit to the ophthalmologist at the local medical center. I accompanied Nick to the doctor's office because his mother couldn't get off work, and I wanted to be certain that the doctor understood the situation. After a thorough examination, the doctor reported that Nick had a very slight astigmatism (an irregularity in the shape of the eye's lens), but that there was nothing wrong with his vision. There was no medical explanation for his red, watery eyes.

Shortly thereafter, I mentioned Nick's problem to a friend, Diane Herrera Shepard, who teaches college students who have learning disabilities. Diane visited my classroom and talked to my students about light sensitivity. After her presentation, she gave Nick a blue transparency to place over the page of his textbook while he was reading. I have to admit I was skeptical, but it worked. Nick read for thirty minutes without stopping, and his eyes didn't bother him at all. He continued to use the transparency and his grades improved, particularly in reading and math. During his junior year, his reading ability and grades improved enough for him to make plans to attend college, an idea he had rejected previously because reading

had been so difficult for him. (At present, he has successfully completed his first three years of college.)

SHEDDING MORE LIGHT ON THE SUBJECT

Nick's experience reminded me of something that had occurred earlier, during my first year as a teacher in California. A young lady had asked for permission to join my
freshman-level English class. Lara had been in special education classes for years and had been diagnosed as having
a severe learning disability that prevented her from reading at grade level, but she said she was ready to join the
"regular" kids. She had just gotten a new pair of glasses—
with blue lenses—and her reading skills improved dramatically. At the time, I didn't realize that the blue lenses
were designed to address her scotopic sensitivity. Lara
transferred to another school shortly thereafter, and I lost
touch with her until three years later when she stopped
by my classroom to report that she was in college studying
to be a special-ed teacher!

After Lara's and Nick's positive experience with the
transparencies, I added a brief discussion of scotopic sensitivity to the presentation on learning styles that I give to students in all of my classes. I've read the arguments against
scotopic sensitivity (many doctors and therapists insist that
it's entirely ridiculous) and I don't advocate the testing, but
I do tell my students that I want them to be aware that the
testing is available if they want to try it. If it helps a student
succeed, I'm willing to accept the criticism.

Last year, here in New Mexico, I had another student, a

freshman named Regina, whose behavior was so similar to Nick's that I made an exception and recommended her for testing. Regina was bright, articulate, and earned high grades, but whenever I assigned independent reading she became a problem child. She would insist that she had to visit the rest room and would be gone for ten or fifteen minutes. If I refused to allow her to leave the room, she'd fidget and squirm, wind her watch, doodle on her notebook, disrupt other students, or try to draw me into conversation. When I pointed out that she only caused these problems during reading, she'd claim that she hated reading, always had, always would. I knew it wasn't a matter of intelligence or ability. On the few occasions that Regina had agreed to read aloud during class, she read very well, although after a few moments, she'd begin to stumble over words, shake her head, rub her eyes, and refuse to continue.

Because I had a handful of students in Regina's class who acted the same way she did during reading, I asked a counselor to visit my classroom and explain scotopic sensitivity to my entire class. The counselor brought some sample worksheets with her and asked for volunteers to be "tested." Regina was first in line. The counselor showed her a page that had a picture of a pumpkin on it. The pumpkin was created by a series of X's, all the same size. Regina's task was to count the number of X's in one particular line of the pumpkin without using her finger to point. Everybody crowded around Regina's desk. Regina couldn't do it. Neither could half of the other students. The rest could easily count off the X's. (By the way, I couldn't count them without pointing, either).

Regina asked for permission to be tested. She took an eye exam and received her parents' permission. I excused her from class for thirty minutes. When she returned, she was carrying three purple transparencies, which she placed over the page we were reading in her literature book. I couldn't even see the print through the transparencies, but Regina was able to read smoothly and correctly. She read until the bell rang and became a regular reading volunteer.

Shortly after Regina was tested, our school counselors gave a presentation to the staff about scotopic sensitivity. Several teachers offered their own experiences. "I used to think I was romantic," one English teacher said, "because I always turn off half the lights in my classroom and at home I have very subdued lighting. Now I realize it's because I need dim lighting in order to read well."

One teacher reported that his daughter—a very successful student—insisted that the only place she could read comfortably was by the dim blue light of the family's tropical fish aquarium. Another teacher introduced a student who told about his own struggles in school, avoiding reading whenever possible, until he had been tested and given a pair of glasses with colored lenses. "Now I'm an A student and going to college next year," the boy explained. "I just wish I had known about this four years ago when school was so much harder for me."

I am far from expert on the subject, but from my reading and discussions with people who are well-educated about light sensitivity, I have learned that there are some clues that frequently indicate a good candidate for testing:

- preference for reading in dim or blue light
- inability to focus under fluorescent lighting
- difficulty reading because of glare from glossy or shiny pages

- black print seems to "float up" off a white page
- the eyes focus on rivers of white between words instead of on the printed words

If you suspect that your child may be sensitive to light, but testing is unavailable or you can't afford testing, you might try changing the environment where your child reads. Try using a 20-watt or 40-watt lightbulb instead of 60 or 100 watts. Try replacing the white lightbulb in his or her lamp with a pink or blue bulb. If you're using fluorescent lights, try switching to incandescent—or vice versa. You might also want to consider trying a full-spectrum lightbulb, which provides light that approximates natural sunlight.

For more information about light sensitivity, contact the nurse or counseling office at your school, or the reference librarian at a public or university library. Another possible source of information is the Dyslexia Treatment and Counseling Center, 940 Saratoga Avenue, San Jose, CA 95129, phone 408-241-3330.

THERE'S NO SUCH THING AS NORMAL

The most important thing to remember about educating children is that every child is an individual who instinctively knows how to learn. If we watch them and truly listen to them—and resist the temptation to insist that they must learn "the right way"—we will learn how to help them learn.

Chapter 4

CHART YOUR CHILD'S PROGRESS

SET UP A SYSTEM

One of the best ways to monitor your child's progress in school is to create your own file system. It may seem like overkill at first, but it's worth your time to keep track of major assignments, reports, exams, report cards, and credits earned. Here's why:

1. You will be showing your child that you believe schoolwork is important.
2. You help build children's confidence when you take their work seriously.
3. You can see immediately when grades go up or down.

4. Maintaining a file system teaches your child valuable organizational skills.
5. You will have a record if there is ever a question about report card grades.

THE LOGISTICS

Your file system doesn't have to be complicated. In fact, it needs to be easy enough to use so that once it is set up, your child can do the filing. The point is not to make extra work, but to keep a record of progress. The simplest approach is to collect your child's papers and keep them until you get the report card for that particular grading period. It doesn't really matter whether you stuff the papers into an envelope or file them neatly in chronological order—the important thing is to keep a record of your child's work so that there is visible proof of progress toward a goal, and to avoid surprises or errors when it's time for grades to be issued.

If your budget is tight, you could buy large binder clips or giant paper clips to hold papers together. Or you could store them in a large manila envelope. This would work well for very young children. For older elementary children, you could use one envelope for each subject area, such as math, science, reading.

Three-ring binders also work well, especially for older students. You could use one big binder with separators for different subjects. When the binder gets full, label it to show what dates it covers and start a new binder. Or you could use one binder for each subject, and keep the same binder for an entire semester or year.

If you're a master organizer, and you have room for a small file cabinet, you might want to use file folders and set up a regular filing system just as administrative secretaries do. File folders allow easy access to papers and can be rearranged, if necessary. You can use folders of different colors or brightly colored labels to identify different subjects. If you have a large family, you could use green folders for one student, yellow for another.

AFTER THE FACT

If storage space is limited at your home, you will probably want to discard everything except special assignments (reports, research papers, essays) after report cards arrive. But if you have the space, I would recommend keeping your student files. In many European countries, students routinely save their notebooks to use as references from one school year to the next. In addition to providing a ready reference, work from previous years also provides a solid record of progress from one year to the next. Students can see the improvement in their basic skills, such as writing and spelling. They also have a record of achievement in subjects such as mathematics, where each year builds upon the previous year's knowledge, with increasingly sophisticated and difficult assignments. What a boost to the ego for a child to be able to see his or her success recorded on paper!

PROGRESS CHARTS

Can you remember the first time you took a difficult math course? Chances are that you opened the book, glanced quickly at a couple of pages in the middle, and decided that you could never learn "all that hard junk." The same thing happens to many students when they enter middle school or high school. They look at the list of graduation requirements and shake their heads, certain that they will never be able to complete everything in time to graduate. For those students, a progress chart works wonders.

I first created a progress chart for a class of at-risk students who were used to failing English. Every day, they asked to see my grade book, to make sure they were still passing. Ryan Winters was always the first in line. He'd rush into my classroom, drop his backpack on a desk, and ask to see his grades in my book. For a few weeks, I showed him. Then, one day, I was busy doing something else and didn't feel like being interrupted.

"I just showed you yesterday," I told Ryan. "You had an 86 percent average. That's a solid B. Do you think your grade mysteriously dropped to a C or D overnight?"

"No," Ryan said, "but I want to check."

"Why?" I asked.

"I just need to see for myself," Ryan insisted. I was about to tell him to be quiet and sit down, but I happened to glance up and see the look on his face. He was telling the truth. He needed to see that grade book, and he needed to see it now. That evening, I took a large piece of manila posterboard, about 2½ by 3 feet, and listed all of the students in Ryan's class down the left-hand side of the paper. I drew a horizontal line across the page, creating a row for each student. Then I drew vertical lines, ½ inch apart, dividing the rest of the paper into sections. (For those visual learners in the crowd, I'll include a copy of this chart.) Now I had a page with a series of forty or so boxes after each student's name. Above the top row of boxes, I listed every assignment I had given Ryan's class. Then I placed a large X in the box for every student who had completed the assignment. For those who were absent, I outlined the box in green. For those who didn't do the work, I placed a big red zero in the box.

The next day, I showed the chart to the students in Ryan's class. They all scrambled to check their rows. Even the kids who insisted they didn't care about grades took their turns checking out the chart. Those who had green squares wanted to know if they could still turn in the work. Those with red zeroes wanted to erase them—I told them I'd give them one break, since it was our first day using the chart. I whited out the zeroes and replaced them with green squares. Everybody had until the end of the week to make up missing assignments. After that, there would be no late work accepted after the final deadline for a specific assignment.

The chart didn't contain any grades, because I don't think it's a good idea to try to create competition for grades to motivate kids. Some people simply can't spell, for example, and all it does is make them feel like failures if you constantly compare them to other people. I wanted my students to compete with themselves—to make sure there was an X in every box. It worked. The students in my other class periods insisted that I make charts for them, too, and everybody (even my "underachievers") started turning in work and making up missed assignments and exams to avoid those big red zeroes. Instead of giving up when they fell behind, or haphazardly turning in assignments without knowing how many they had missed, my students knew exactly where they stood and what they needed to do to earn a passing grade. At the end of that semester, every single student in my classes passed English!

WHY AM I TELLING YOU THIS?

You may be wondering, *Why is she telling me this? I can't possibly keep track of every single assignment and exercise my child does in school.* That's true. It would be impractical at best, most likely impossible, for you to keep track of every single assignment and exercise your child does in school. Not all assignments are graded; some are designed to allow students to practice new skills. I shared that story with you because it taught me the importance of showing children some visible sign of their progress. They also need to see how many assignments they have completed and how many they have missed. Many students who didn't seem to care about their grades became very interested when they could see the line of check marks moving toward a goal—a passing grade. It seems logical to me that even if you don't have all the assignments for a given class or subject, if you keep the ones that are graded and returned to your child, you will have a pretty good sense of what's happening in school.

THE BIG PICTURE

I also told you about the progress chart because it led to another kind of chart, one that you can make and use at home to help motivate your child. At the end of the first semester using our progress charts, one of my seniors came to my classroom in tears. For several minutes, she was unable to speak because she was sobbing so hard. When she finally calmed down, she told me that she was not going to be able to walk in the graduation ceremony for her class because she was one-half credit short of the graduation requirements for our school district.

"I failed one quarter of science in my freshman year," she said, "and I was supposed to make it up, but nobody ever told me and they never scheduled it for me and I forgot about it."

Although I suspected that one of the guidance counselors had probably told Tiffany she needed to make up the credit, that wasn't the point. Without that half credit, she couldn't graduate. She could make up the work during summer school and receive her diploma in the mail, but she had had her heart set on graduating with her classmates.

Determined to avoid another case like Tiffany's, I asked the guidance office to provide me with transcripts for all of my students. I drew a large poster listing the district graduation requirements and hung it on the wall in my classroom. Then I used my computer to create a simple form that listed every requirement (my form is included, but you will need to customize your form to coincide with your child's school requirements, which may be different). I made one copy of the form for each student. We spent one class period going over the transcripts and checking off the completed courses from the list of requirements. When we finished, we filed the transcripts and lists in manila folders and kept them until the next report cards were issued and transcripts were updated.

You can do the same at home. Most schools provide a student handbook (which students rarely read) that lists graduation requirements. Some schools mail them to parents. But most people glance through the handbook, toss it in the trash, or file it away and forget about it.

For middle and high school students, if you don't receive a handbook, you can ask the guidance office for a copy of the student's transcript. Check to make sure the grades on the transcript and the report card match. Make sure the number of credits is accurate. If there is any error, write a brief note explaining the discrepancy and mail or deliver it to the proper guidance counselor (sometimes they are assigned by grade level). Follow up in two weeks. If the correction hasn't been made, follow up every week until it is corrected. If it takes the people in the office a while to respond, don't assume it's because they don't care. Instead, assume they are busy and it's easy to lose track of one child's credits among the piles of paperwork in any school office.

PUT RESPONSIBILITY ON THE STUDENT

Yes, it is the school's responsibility to provide necessary classes, to schedule students into those classes, to provide instruction, and to accurately record grades. But if

Sample

John's Progress Chart				
Class: English		Teacher: Ms. Jordan		Period: 4th
	Completed assignment	Took test	Incomplete	Didn't do it
Spelling #1	X			
Vocabulary test		X		
Pop quiz		X		
Journal #1			√	
Book report			√	
Vocabulary test		X		
Journal #2				O
Spelling #2			√	
Midterm		X		
Vocabulary test			√	
Journal #3				O
Spelling #3	X			
Essay			√	
Journal #4	X			
Pop quiz		X		

Sample Progress Chart

Legend:
- x = done
- □ = missing
- ☒ = made up
- ○ = no credit

Name	Spelling quiz #1	Vocabulary worksheet #1	Vocabulary quiz #1	Journal #1	Literature worksheet	Spelling quiz #2	Journal #2	Literature essay	Vocabulary worksheet #2	Vocabulary quiz #2		
Abdul-Haqq, C.	x	x	x	x	x	x	x	x	x	x		
Aguito, E.	x	☒	x	x	☒	○	x	x	□	x		
Anderson, M.	x	x	x	○	x	☒	x	x	x	□		
Banaag, T.	□	x	x	x	x	x	x	□	x	x		
Bendetto, S.	x	x	x	x	x	x	x	x	x	x		
Bonner, R.	x	x	○	○	x	x	○	x	☒	☒		
Burns, T.	x	x	x	x	☒	x	x	x	x	x		
Carter, M.	x	x	x	○	x	x	x	☒	x	x		
Chavez, M.	x	x	x	x	x	x	x	x	x	□		
Chu, M.	x	x	x	x	x	☒	x	x	x	x		
Davis, S.												
DiDonato, V.												
Ellison, R.												
Farhang, E.												

4th period

English II

Your High School District Graduation Requirements

Note: This form is set up for a quarter schedule. If your school uses semesters, or a different credit count, you will need to change the form.

Very important: Check your transcript against your report card to make sure you received credit for every class completed. If there is an error, or if you failed a class, make a note under "Remarks" and be sure to follow up.

Each X = ____ quarter credits. Place an X on the blank for each quarter you pass a course.

Quarter:	9th grade 1 2 3 4	10th grade 1 2 3 4	11th grade 1 2 3 4	12th grade 1 2 3 4	Remarks
English total (__)	_ _ _ _	_ _ _ _	_ _ _ _	_ _ _ _	_____
Math total (__)	_ _ _ _	_ _ _ _	_ _ _ _	_ _ _ _	_____
Science total (__)	_ _ _ _	_ _ _ _	_ _ _ _	_ _ _ _	_____
Social Studies total (__)	_ _ _ _	_ _ _ _	_ _ _ _	_ _ _ _	_____
Physical Education total (__)	_ _ _ _	_ _ _ _	_ _ _ _	_ _ _ _	_____
Fine Arts total (__)	_ _ _ _	_ _ _ _	_ _ _ _	_ _ _ _	_____

Electives
(total____) (List name of each course and write date completed when you check it off.)

_____   _ _ _ _   _____

_____   _ _ _ _   _____

_____   _ _ _ _   _____

_____   _ _ _ _   _____

================

_____ **Total credits required for graduation** (be sure you use the correct number for your school).

Your High School District Graduation Requirements

Note: This form is set up for a semester schedule. If your school uses quarters, you will need to use the other form.

Very important: Check your transcript against your report card to make sure you received credit for every class completed. If there is an error, or if you failed a class, make a note under "Remarks" and be sure to follow up.

Each X = _____ semester credits. Place an X on the blank for each semester you pass a course.

	9th grade 1 2	10th grade 1 2	11th grade 1 2	12th grade 1 2	Remarks
English total (__)	__ __	__ __	__ __	__ __	_____
Math total (__)	__ __	__ __	__ __	__ __	_____
Science total (__)	__ __	__ __	__ __	__ __	_____
Social Studies total (__)	__ __	__ __	__ __	__ __	_____
Physical Education total (__)	__ __	__ __	__ __	__ __	_____
Fine Arts total (__)	__ __	__ __	__ __	__ __	_____

Electives (total_____) (List name of each course and write date completed when you check it off.)

_____ _____ _____

_____ _____ _____

_____ _____ _____

_____ _____ _____

_____

_____ **Total credits required for graduation** (be sure you use the correct number for your school).

Your High School District Graduation Requirements

Note: This form is set up for a semester schedule and five credits per course each semester. If your school uses quarters or some other term division, or counts one credit per course, you will need to change this form accordingly.

Very important: Check your transcript against your report card to make sure you received credit for every class completed. If there is an error, or if you failed a class, make a note under "Remarks" and be sure to follow up.

Each X = 5 semester credits. Place an X on the blank for each semester you pass a course.

	9th grade		10th grade		11th grade		12th grade		Remarks
	1	2	1	2	1	2	1	2	
English total (40)	—	—	—	—	—	—	—	—	_____
Math total (30)	—	—	—	—	—	—	—	—	_____
Science total (30)	—	—	—	—	—	—	—	—	_____
Social Studies total (40)	—	—	—	—	—	—	—	—	_____
Physical Education total (40)	—	—	—	—	—	—	—	—	_____
Fine Arts total (20)	—	—	—	—	—	—	—	—	_____

Electives
(total 20) (List name of each course and write date completed when you check it off.)

_____ _____ _____

_____ _____ _____

_____ _____ _____

_____ _____ _____

_____

<u>220</u> **Total credits required for graduation** (be sure you use the correct number for your school).

the school employees make a mistake, it's the child who isn't promoted to the next grade level, or who doesn't graduate on time. I tell my students, "It may be this school's job to provide your education, but it is your job to make sure you get that education. Keep track of your credits. Make sure you are scheduled into the classes you need. Take responsibility for your education and your life. It doesn't matter if somebody else made the mistake—you're the one who will suffer if you don't pay attention."

WHAT ABOUT THE LITTLE GUYS?

I realize that I tend to focus on secondary school students, but nearly everything that works for them can be modified for younger children. Elementary schools usually have a list of requirements that students must complete before they are passed to the next higher grade level. Ask for a copy of the list. When you receive a report card, contact the teacher and the guidance counselor and find out whether your child is making the necessary progress. Take notes during your meetings, and list what your child needs to accomplish in order to be promoted. Then, make a chart that lists the skills and activities required during the quarter or semester. Hang the chart where your child can see it. Circle the areas that need extra attention, such as spelling, writing sentences, following verbal instructions, and so on. Each time you spend one-half hour working on a particular skill or practicing an activity, put a check mark in the proper column. At the end of the report card period, write down on the chart the grade earned for each subject or area. Paste gold or silver stars on the good grades, and encourage your child to work on raising the low grades to "star level." (We'll talk about what constitutes a "good" grade in a moment.)

MAKE SCHOOL A BIG DEAL

Probably the most important part of monitoring progress is rewarding good behavior, sincere effort, and passing grades. I'll spend more time later talking about using rewards to motivate kids who hate school. Right now, I'd like to suggest that you make a big deal of acknowledging your child's achievements at the end of every grading period. Rewards don't have to be elaborate or expensive. Shake their hands and tell them how proud you are, just as you would an adult who had achieved a difficult goal. Make a favorite dessert for dinner. Invite a close friend for a sleep-over. Hold an awards ceremony in your living room and videotape it. Invite the neighbors over for cookies, juice, and a round of applause for the successful student. Let your child choose a "grownup pen" from the local stationers to use at school. Surprise your child with a favorite audio tape or CD. Write a note saying how proud you are and leave the note on the child's pillow.

The end of a school year is an exciting time for children, a perfect opportunity for you to create more excitement about education. Even if your child's school holds a ceremony to recognize students' achievements, I still recommend holding your own personal ceremony or celebration at home. Make paper hats. Make "graduation robes" out of sheets. Design your own certificates. Bake a cake. Take photos. Make your kids feel special for having moved through an important milestone in their young lives. I know, I know—teenagers will roll their eyes and protest that it's "so stupid," but they will secretly enjoy the attention and recognition. Wouldn't you?

SHOULD WE PAY KIDS FOR GOOD GRADES?

I wish I had the answer to that question. It's a good question, and one that I am asked frequently. I've heard many arguments, both for and against this idea. My answer is, "It depends." It depends on your relationship with your child, your bank account, and your child's personality and maturity.

If your child demands money for a good grade, and threatens not to work in school if you don't pay, then I think it would be a big mistake to pay your child. Money for grades should be considered a bonus, not something you owe your child. Imagine how your boss would react if he or she offered you a bonus for achieving a particular goal at work, and you threatened not to work at all if you didn't receive the bonus. You probably wouldn't get the bonus, and you might lose your job.

The payment for working in school is a good education. You can't put a price tag on that, nor can you place a dollar value on having a good, solid work ethic. One of the best gifts we can give our children is the joy of achieving a goal. We need to help them discover how wonderful it feels to know they've done their best at whatever task they have been given, even if they aren't wildly successful. The only true failure is in not trying.

Perhaps your parents (or grandparents) paid you for good grades on your report card, and you turned out to be a wonderful adult. In that case, you may want to pay your children for good grades. If you can afford it, why not do it? (I would ask one question—are you going to reward the child who worked very hard to earn a B or C, just as you would one who earned an A?) If you do pay your children, you have the opportunity to teach them about money management. I don't think it's a good idea to give a lot of cash to children, unless they have the self-control to save at least some of it. I'd suggest letting them spend part of the money, and putting the rest into a savings account. Some parents give savings bonds or other rewards that don't involve money.

I lied to you. I said I didn't have an answer to the question of whether to pay children for grades. I do have an answer, although it's only my opinion. After watching thousands of students respond to their report cards, and seeing the way those students react to their parents' response to those report cards, I don't think money is the best motivator. I think the reward that children most appreciate is a hug, a handshake, a pat on the back, and the words "I am so proud of you."

ONE REWARD IS WORTH A THOUSAND PUNISHMENTS

Unfortunately, disruptive students are like the proverbial squeaky wheels—they get most of our attention. Even when we try to give equal time to all the children, the ones who misbehave demand our immediate attention. Then there are the superstudents, the kids who are responsible, studious, cooperative, and considerate of others. We thank them, reward them, and so on. Which leaves very little time for the kids in the middle, the ones who behave most of the time and earn passing grades.

Most kids fall into the middle category, but they get the least attention. When I started teaching, I was determined to treat all my students equally, and I thought I did, until one of my students forced me to look at myself. Melanie was an above average student, rarely absent, usually cooperative, and willing to work with any group of classmates. Overnight, without warning, Melanie turned into a teacher's nightmare. She stopped turning in her homework and started causing all kinds of trouble during class—talking loudly to distract other kids, throwing paper, refusing to complete her assignments, interrupting me when I was talking to the class. At first, I ignored her, hoping she would grow tired of her game, but she didn't. When I asked her to stay after school for a meeting, I expected her to shrug her shoulders and refuse to talk to me. But, when I asked Melanie what had happened to make her act the way she had been acting lately, she looked me straight in the eye and told me.

"I've been going to school for ten years," she said. "And I've been a good little girl all that time. I never got in trouble. I never flunked any classes. I never had to go to the office. But I never won any awards either, and nobody paid any attention to me. Sometimes my teachers would mark me absent when I was there because I was quiet. And sometimes they would forget to mark me absent when I was home sick because they didn't miss me when I wasn't there. I just got tired of it. So I decided to act like the kids that everybody notices. Now everybody knows my name. I get in trouble a lot, but at least the teachers notice me now. And so do the other kids."

When Melanie left my room, I sat down at my desk and went over my roll sheets, counting the number of "good kids" like her. Six or seven out of every ten kids fit the category. Then I tried to remember how many times I had rewarded those kids for coming to class, co-operating with me, and staying out of trouble. I couldn't remember very many. I felt so ashamed of myself. The next day, I announced to all of my classes that I was sorry I hadn't been fair to the kids who didn't cause trouble in class. I thanked them for their good behavior and told them how much I appreciated it. During class, I made a special point of stopping by the desks of the cooperative students and patting them on the shoulder, or giving them a special smile. At the end of each class, I stood by the door and said, "Thank you so much for your cooperation. You know who I'm talking to, and so do I. I truly appreciate your good behavior. It has been a distinct pleasure being your teacher today and I look forward to the next opportunity." They laughed at me, but I could tell that they appreciated my appreciation. After that, I made sure I truly did pay equal attention to all of my students.

By the way, some of Melanie's other teachers joined with me in making sure we spoke to her every day, and thanked her when she behaved. Before long, she returned to her former cheerful, likable self. She hadn't misbehaved long enough to cause any serious damage to her overall grade point average, but I certainly learned my lesson. And I have seen other students who weren't as lucky as Melanie; when they decide to become "bad kids," nobody intervenes in time to stop them from self-destructing. It's important to notice good behavior and thank children for it. If we don't reward them, what incentive do they have for continuing to be good?

A'S ARE NICE, BUT THEY AREN'T EVERYTHING

On my first day in the classroom, one of my students informed me that he knew I wouldn't like him. I said I thought I might. "Not when you see my grades," he said with a huge sigh. "Nobody likes me when they see my grades."

Another student, Richie Ferrigno, an outgoing young man with a dynamic personality, once accused me of liking another student more than I liked him. At first, I thought he was kidding, but I soon realized he was serious. When I insisted that I liked all my students equally well, Richie shook his head.

"No, you don't," Richie said. "You like Violeta and Eric and Shamica better because they get A's in everything. But all the teachers are like that, so I'm used to it by now."

Richie's comments sparked a class discussion, which made me realize he wasn't the only kid in class who believed I (and all the other teachers) liked the students with high grades the most. It took me quite a long time to convince them that I was sincere, that I liked them as people, in spite of their grades.

"Naturally, I am happy when you earn a good grade," I explained, "but that doesn't mean I like you any less if you earn a low grade. When you get a low grade, I feel sad, but I still like you just as much. Maybe even more, because it means you aren't perfect—you are human. A low grade just means you need to work harder at learning or that the teacher needs to work harder at teaching."

Richie and his pals aren't unusual. Most children believe that grades are an indication of their worth as human beings. They also believe that adults like them better when they earn good grades. We need to make sure they understand that we like them regardless of their grades.

An A Isn't Always an A   Just as children tend to believe that students who earn A's are better, more likable people, most of them believe that kids who earn A's are the smartest kids in class. Maybe they are, but maybe they aren't. I don't think good grades necessarily indicate high intelligence. They don't indicate worth as a human being. They don't indicate ability to learn. They don't indicate how much you can learn if you try.

Sometimes good grades *do* indicate intelligence, but often they indicate natural talent, hard work, luck, or a combination of those three. I would bet that you know people who earned straight A's in school, but who can't solve the simplest problems in life and have no friends when they are grown up. We also know people who earned very poor grades in school, but who are very successful and popular as adults. I think it's important to keep grades in their proper perspective. A's are very nice, but they aren't everything. I believe it is just as important to be an "A person"—honest, ethical, loyal, hardworking—as it is to have good grades. And I would much rather have an A child who earns F's in school than an F person who earns A's. You can always work to raise a grade, but it's next to impossible to turn an obnoxious, unethical, lazy person into a good citizen.

Speaking of IQ   A few years ago, at a community meeting here in Las Cruces, I had the good fortune to hear a speech by Lowell Catlett, a professor from New Mexico State University. Professor Catlett explained that when Albert Einstein died, research scientists studied his brain, hoping to discover the cause of his superior intelligence. Apparently, they discovered that Einstein's brain contained a much higher amount of a certain chemical than normal brains do. Some people immediately jumped to the conclusion that abundance of this chemical explained the man's intelligence. Further studies indicated that sustained hard thinking would cause the brain to create the chemical in question, therefore posing the possibility that we humans can "think ourselves smarter." It makes sense to me. I have had many students who weren't supposed to be smart, who started at the bottom of the class and ended up at the top as a result of hard work and faith in themselves. They didn't accept the idea that there was a limit to their intelligence. They believed they could be just as smart as they wanted to be.

What's So Bad About C's?   Somewhere along the line, a perfectly respectable C became a mark of shame. Instead of accepting that not everybody is good at everything, we began to believe that all children needed to excel at everything. That's not realistic, and it's not fair to children.

Of course, kids need to earn good grades. We should encourage them to succeed, but what's wrong with earning C's? What's wrong with making a few mistakes, learning more than 70 percent of some new information, or being able to perform a new skill adequately enough to complete a given task? How can we expect children to try their hardest if they know we will be disappointed when they aren't perfect? I'm not saying that we should tell children to do their best and then accept whatever they do the first time around as the best they can do. But what's wrong with trying something new, failing, and trying again?

We know some of the reasons why C's fell from grace. For many years, only students with straight A's were accepted into colleges and universities. In response to pressure from students and parents, some high school administrations began to encourage teachers to lower their standards or inflate their students' grades. Because more students bring more tuition dollars, many colleges and universities couldn't afford to turn away students whose performance on campus fell far short of their inflated high school grades.

But I think the primary reason the C stopped being acceptable had more to do with self-esteem than money. When research studies revealed that self-esteem and teachers' expectations had more to do with success in the classroom than IQ scores, some adults thought the answer would be to make every child feel like an A student. They created "success experiences" wherein every child achieved the same high grade or result. But kids aren't stupid. When you give them high grades for anything less than true effort and achievement, they don't feel good about themselves. They feel cheated. They believe they were given a grade, or that a success was created for them because they weren't capable of earning it themselves. They don't feel better about themselves when they participate in an exercise that is designed to make everybody feel smart—they know exactly what's happening, and they think that the reason they were given the exercise was because they were too stupid to face a real challenge.

One more question, and I'll get off my soapbox and get on with it. *Why does everybody have to be good at everything?* There are things I do very well—dance, for example—and things I do fairly well, such as play the piano. There are some things I do quite poorly, such as balance my checkbook, and there are some things I can't do at all (although I prefer to believe that I don't really want to do those things). The reason I don't feel badly about my poor performance in some areas is that I know if I really wanted to, I could work to improve those areas. I have confidence in my ability to learn. That's what we need to give our children—confidence that they can learn. With confidence comes self-esteem, and children who possess those two things succeed in school and in life. Honest assessment of their performance, an opportunity to make mistakes without penalty, and encouragement to continue trying—those things will help children much more than report cards filled with high grades that they know they didn't really earn.

Nobody's Perfect　Maybe students who earn C averages aren't going to be accepted into Ivy League schools immediately following high school graduation. That doesn't mean they can't be successful people. Or that they won't decide later on to go to college and earn very high grades.

Older college students often excel because they have some experience in the workplace and they discover that they can achieve goals, that they are just as smart as many of their coworkers—often smarter than their supervisors.

On the other hand, a straight-A high school record doesn't guarantee success in college. When I taught composition at New Mexico State University, my first class was an honors level freshman composition class; all of the students had high grade point averages from high school, and most were on academic scholarships. By the end of the first semester, nearly half of the students in that class had lost their scholarships—not because they weren't smart enough to do the work, but because they had never had to work hard in school before. They were used to earning A's with little effort. Several of them confided to me that they had never failed at anything in their lives. When they earned anything less than an A, they were so upset and disillusioned that they gave up. They had never learned how to fail, or how to use failure as a stepping stone to success.

Who Says You Have to Want an A?   Every student should want an A. That's what I thought when I started teaching. So, when Chris Lindell, a very intelligent young man, did only the minimum required to earn a C, I was concerned. I talked to Chris. I talked to his parents. I talked to the counselors. We all agreed that Chris had the brains and ability to earn an A in English if he wanted to. But Chris didn't want to.

"Why does he have to want an A?" my supervisory teacher and mentor, Hal Gray, asked me when I complained to him about Chris's lack of motivation. "What's wrong with a C?"

"Nothing's wrong with it," I said, "but he could earn an A."

"Well, maybe he doesn't want an A," Hal said.

"But he should want an A," I insisted.

"Why?" Hal asked.

"Because he can earn one if he wants to," I explained, exasperated by Hal's seeming stupidity. "If you can earn an A, you should want one."

"Who are you to decide what Chris should want?" Hal said.

"I'm his teacher," I said. "And you're supposed to be my teacher. You aren't helping me."

"And you aren't helping Chris," Hal said. "The boy is a talented musician, good enough that professional jazz bands let him sit in and play his trumpet with them sometimes."

"That's not more important than school," I said.

"Why not?" Hal asked. "It's more important to Chris. But even though he doesn't think high school is important, he's willing to come here every day, do the work we give him, and earn passing grades. I think that's pretty mature behavior for a sixteen-year-old kid. A lot of teenagers with his kind of talent would just quit coming to school."

It took a while, but Hal's message finally sank in. Chris had a right to choose his grades. If he was satisfied with C's, then why couldn't I be satisfied with them? Did I think he was going to be an abject failure in his life if he didn't earn A's in English and history during high school? Maybe not, but I was afraid he might regret his behavior later on. What if he decided he wanted to go to college after graduation and couldn't get into a good school? I mentioned my concern to Hal and he suggested I talk to Chris about it.

"I know I might be sorry later on," Chris said, "but isn't that part of growing up, learning from your mistakes? Maybe life will be harder for me later. I realize that, but this is the choice I want to make right now. I don't really care about school and I don't think I'll need all this stuff I'm learning, but everybody tells me I'll be sorry if I don't get my diploma, people I trust, like you and my parents. So I'm going to finish school. But I just don't want to take the time away from my music to get A's and B's."

I didn't argue with him.

An A Can be Scary   At the end of one semester, grades in my sophomore English class began to plummet. Students who had earned A's and B's for weeks were now skipping homework assignments and failing exams. I reminded them frequently that their grades were slipping, but that there was still time to make up the lost work. Only a few took me up on my offer.

"It's almost as though they're trying not to earn A's," I told the assistant principal. "It sounds crazy, but I'm positive that some of them are sabotaging their own grades."

Dr. Horner nodded. "I've seen it happen before," he said. "You get a kid who doesn't earn A's as a rule. Then he starts to work, sees an A in the grade book, and panics. He's afraid of that A. If he takes home a report card with an A on it, maybe his parents will expect an A every time, or an A in every subject. He's afraid he won't be able to keep up the level of effort, or that he's not really smart enough to earn A's all the time. Or maybe his parents will now expect him to go to college and he doesn't want to go. He knows he can earn an A. He's done it. But he doesn't want anybody else to know, so he makes sure they don't find out."

Dr. Horner also said he had seen students, both boys and girls, who had been beaten up by other students for "making them look bad." And sometimes brothers and sisters put pressure on a child not to set too high a standard of achievement.

There are a lot of reasons why children choose the grades they earn. If we want to convince them to earn the grades we want them to have, we first have to understand why they chose the lower grades in the first place.

Don't worry that your children will stop trying if you don't push them to earn good grades. Encourage them to work hard, by all means. But if you push, don't be surprised if they push back twice as hard.

WHAT SHOULD I SAY?

"What should I say?" one mother asked me when I suggested that she avoid putting too much pressure on her daughter but still encourage her daughter to earn the highest possible grades. "I'm not very good at this," she said. "Whenever I bring up the subject of grades, Shirmel accuses me of yelling at her."

I wrote down my "speech" for Shirmel's mother, but suggested that she reword it so it would sound more natural to her and her daughter. It goes something like this:

I would be very happy if you earned an A, but I will also be happy if you earn a B or a C. I will love you just as much, no matter what grade you earn, even a failing grade. If you earn a D or an F, I will still love you, but I will help you study and work to raise your grade so you can be successful in school. It's important to do your best work all the time, at home and at school, to be proud of every job you do, but nobody is perfect. Everybody makes mistakes. That's how we learn. Everybody can learn, including you. So do your best. That's all you can do. I am proud of you for being the wonderful, unique person that you are, and I will like you no matter what grades you earn. I am happy when you succeed, and sad when you fail, because I have failed myself and I know that it hurts. But I also know that I have learned so much from my mistakes, and I know you will learn from yours. The most important thing is to try. You can still be an A person, even if your grades aren't always perfect. If you need help, tell me. If I can't help you, I'll find somebody who can.

KIDS WILL STILL TRY

My remedial freshman English class hated school. These weren't dumb kids. There was nothing wrong with their brains, but they earned very poor grades and hated school with a passion. They hated reading and writing, but what they hated most of all was tests. Even when they knew the material—and I knew they knew it—they didn't seem to be able to earn good test scores.

One day I decided to try a different approach. I closed

my grade book and announced that I no longer cared what grades they earned. Any passing grade would do. From that day on, we would have two "practice exams" before any "real exam" would be given.

"Don't you want us to get A's?" one of the girls asked.

"That would be nice," I said, "but only if you want an A. I'll be just as happy if you earn a B or a C."

"What about D's?" one boy wanted to know.

"Well, I'll be concerned about D's, because it won't leave you any safety net if you get sick or mess up on a test. And if you fail my class, it means I have failed as a teacher, and I don't want that to happen. So if you earn a D, I'm going to work with you on the material."

So, we started using "practice exams." Students had the option of keeping the grade from the first practice test if it was a 75 percent (C) or above. If they opted to take the second practice or the "real test," and somehow earned a lower score, they could still keep the grade from the first "practice" test. I knew they thought I had lost my marbles, but they didn't argue with me. The three tests were all different—they didn't contain the same questions, although they covered the same material from the textbook and lectures.

After the first practice exam, a few students chose to keep their C's. They pretended to work on the assignment I gave them while the other students took the second practice and "real" tests. Most of the students improved on the second practice exam, and again on the "real" test. Nobody earned a lower score on the "real" test than they had on the first practice. And nobody failed to pass the second practice exam.

It was obvious as I looked out across the classroom during the "real test" period that the kids were more relaxed. They weren't worried about their grades because they had that practice grade to fall back on. The worst that could happen was that they would pass with a C. Not bad for a worst-case scenario.

By the third test cycle, everybody was repeating tests, doing makeup assignments, asking for extra credit. The less emphasis I put on grades, the harder they tried to earn A's. They were no longer afraid to take chances, to test their skills, to push themselves a little harder, because they knew it would be all right. If they failed, they could try again.

Those students taught me a very important lesson. They showed me that it is natural for children to strive for success, that they are self-motivated and will strive for perfection as long as we love them when they aren't perfect.

I know it's hard not to push. It was hard for me not to try to influence my students to earn A's. But self-restraint is a valuable skill—and who better to teach us than our children?

Chapter 5

RULES, RESPONSIBILITY, AND REWARDS

RULES CREATE FREEDOM

I like to think of rules as a kind of scaffolding for children. They provide support and keep children from falling and seriously injuring themselves. As children grow older, the rules can be relaxed or removed, one at a time, until the children stand alone, making their own decisions, taking as much risk as their confidence and abilities will allow.

One of the biggest obstacles children face in school is learning to follow rules. One of the best ways you can help your child succeed in school is to create a reasonable framework of rules to follow at home. Children who have no limits at home, who are left to make their own decisions, have a very hard time fitting into the structured environment of the classroom. They can't follow instructions, they resent authority, and they are not concerned with how their own behavior affects others. Often they don't understand why they aren't successful, when they are as intelligent as the other children in the classroom. They think of rules as the enemy, things that spoil all their fun, instead of as a framework that will allow them to learn better and eventually increase their freedoms.

It might seem as though children would enjoy being completely free to do whatever they choose, but that isn't true. Children need rules and guidelines to provide a safety net for them. The world is a big and scary place, even for teenagers, and they look to us to draw the boundaries to keep them safe and help them make decisions. If rules are reasonable and the consequences for breaking them make sense, then children learn that rules can be helpful.

Rules can save time, energy, and pain. For example, if a child had the choice of playing a ball game outside with friends, watching TV, playing computer games, or doing homework, most children would choose to play. Even if they wanted to do their homework, friends might persuade them to skip it, or the dramatic beginning of the TV show might capture their interest and hold them hostage. They would have fun for a while, but the next day they'd suffer. Their teachers would be disappointed, their grades would go down, and their parents would be upset (if they were aware that homework wasn't done). They might be able to make up the work, but sometimes one important assignment can mean the difference between earning a B or C, passing or failing an exam, or even earning a passing grade for a particular subject.

On the other hand, if there was a rule that all home-work must be completed immediately after school or before children could play games, they would not have to make the decision themselves. They would know that they had to do their work first. They would not only earn better grades, but they would also learn so many other valuable things: to set priorities, to manage time effectively, to exercise self-discipline. They would also learn that adults think their schoolwork is important, and that we want them to be successful in school.

It isn't fair to expect children to make so many decisions, at least not about things as important as their education. It also isn't fair to expect them to resist peer pressure all by themselves, especially when they are very young. They don't have the maturity and experience to make sound decisions. They need our help. Of course, they need to be allowed to make decisions for themselves and learn from their mistakes, but there are many other areas in which they could make mistakes that don't involve such long-term risks. What to do with their allowance, experimenting with different recipes, trying out a part-time job, learning how much work is involved in keeping a pet—all of these teach important lessons without jeopardizing a child's education. Sometimes, when a child falls behind in school, he or she spends months or years trying to catch up.

MORE ISN'T BETTER

When it comes to rules, the fewer the better—for adults as well as children. Consider your city and state traffic laws. There are so many laws that very few people bother to follow all of them. We follow the ones we remember or the ones we think are valid and important or the ones we know we will be punished for if we're caught. And I'm sure you know at least one adult who considers a speed limit sign as a challenge to drive just a little bit faster. I'm sure *you* never, ever did anything you weren't supposed to do when you were a child, but I admit that I sometimes tried to see whether I could chew gum in Mr. Miller's science class without getting caught. And once in a while I even fibbed to my parents. One summer, I fell out of a tree; I wasn't hurt, but my mother forbade me to climb trees anymore. Each morning, when I went out to play, I would say, "Mom, I promise not to climb any tree today." What I didn't tell my mother was that my friend Marty and I had named all the trees in our neighborhood—A Tree, Another Tree, The Tree, Any Tree, Marty's Tree, etc. So, technically, I didn't lie to my mother, but I didn't tell the truth either. I didn't think her rule was reasonable, and I was willing to risk getting caught because I enjoyed tree climbing so much. Perhaps there was also just a little bit of a thrill in knowing that I was breaking a rule.

Another disadvantage of making long lists of rules is that you have to remember them! During my first year as a teacher, I made the mistake of creating an incredibly long list of rules, with an accompanying list of punishments for students who broke the rules. My list drove us all crazy. I couldn't remember all the rules, so I didn't always punish the students who broke them, which caused a lot of resentment among the ones who did get caught and punished. Sometimes I couldn't remember the punishments I had assigned, so I didn't administer them fairly and consistently to all students. My rules ended up creating an antagonistic environment—the kids were upset with me and fought with each other. Nobody was happy.

When I explained to my students that I had made a mistake and wanted to design a new set of rules, I thought they might lose respect for me. They didn't. They were relieved.

"Please don't make so many rules next time," one of the girls said. "Just a couple really big ones." The other students agreed: Rules should only include the most important things, things they should never, ever do under any circumstances, such as hit each other. I realized they were right. After much thought, I reduced my rule list to two items:

1. Respect yourself and the other people in this room.
2. No insults against anybody's race, religion, skin color, ethnic background, gender, or sexual preference.

(I realize that rule number 2 would be included under rule number 1, but I wanted to make a special point of prohibiting such insults.) When I first listed my two new, improved rules, one of the boys warned me that they weren't "hard" enough. "You gotta have more rules than that," he said.

"Tell me something bad that you can do that won't break one of those two rules," I said.

"I could stick gum under my desk," he said. "That doesn't insult anybody."

"No," I said, "but it is disrespectful to me, the janitor,

and anybody else who sits at that desk." He tried a few more suggestions, but the other students shouted him down. We agreed to try the two-rule list and see how well it worked. It worked wonderfully and it changed the dynamics in my classroom entirely. Instead of spending so much time on what they couldn't do, the students reminded each other of what they should do. Later, after reading some books about classroom management, I learned that the experts recommend making "positive" rather than "negative" rules. For example, the positive rule, Put all dirty clothes in the hamper, is more effective than its negative counterpart, Don't throw dirty clothes on the floor.

RULES VERSUS PROCEDURES

Another lesson I learned the hard way is the difference between rules and procedures. Rules are rules—inflexible and consistent. Procedures are methods or systems for accomplishing certain tasks or goals. For example, at our home we have a strict rule—No eating while using the computer—and nobody is allowed to break that rule, including the "big kids." We also have procedures for using the computer. We have a fifteen-minute time limit if somebody else is waiting to play games, we keep the sound low if somebody else is watching TV, and we always return to the DOS screen before turning off the main power switch. The primary difference between rules and procedures is that procedures are flexible and can be adapted to fit different individual needs and circumstances.

In my classroom, I used to have a rule that all makeup work had to be completed within two days of a student's returning to class after an absence. Sometimes that simply didn't work. Students who had been seriously ill had too much work to make up. Other times, there was an exam scheduled for the following day, and the students needed to do the missed work immediately in order to be prepared for the exam. So, I changed the rule to a procedure that didn't back me or the student into a corner. Now the procedure for students returning after being absent is to collect their makeup work from the folder on my desk, then discuss the assignments with me and we will determine how much time will be needed to complete the makeup work.

The same idea can work at home, especially for younger children. They enjoy learning to do things the way the "big kids" do. I am not suggesting that you run your home like a military boot camp, but children thrive in an organized environment. They enjoy learning tasks that require specific steps (first, we scrape the leftovers into the dog's dish, then we rinse the plate, then we place the plate in the sink to be washed). They also need to have boundaries set for them, although they will complain and push them to the limit. That's natural. But no matter how hard they push, children don't want us to stop setting limits. I can't tell you how many times a child has confided to me that his or her parents don't care at all. Why do the children believe that? "Because they don't care what happens to me. They let me do anything I want to."

By setting reasonable rules and establishing logical procedures in your home, you show your children that you care about them and you care what kind of people they grow up to be. Also, by setting rules you will be helping your children develop a sense of responsibility, self-discipline, respect for others, and the ability to follow directions. This will help them succeed in school, at college, on the job, and in their personal relationships.

ALL THE OTHER KIDS ARE DOING IT

Persuading kids to cooperate isn't always easy, but a little psychology can work wonders. Once, when I had a particularly resistant group of students, I assigned an exercise I had done in one of my college classes. The professor had designed the "Have to and Can't" exercise to make his students realize how often we tried to place the blame for our unhappiness or dissatisfaction on other people or things. After completing the exercise, I left his class with a new sense of personal responsibility and power. I've done the same assignment with every class of students I've taught, regardless of age, with the same positive results: It helps them realize that they are responsible for their own success and happiness.

Have to and Can't   There are four steps to the "Have to and Can't" exercise. All you need is a pencil and a sheet of paper. Ready?

   1. Write down the following two sentences on your sheet of paper:
      I have to _____. I can't _____.
   2. Finish both sentences with the first thing that comes

to your mind. Don't worry about what you write. This is not a test and people won't see your answers unless you show them.

3. Cross out the words *have to* and write *choose to* above them. Now read your new sentence to yourself and decide which sentence is true.

4. Cross out the word *can't* and write *don't want to* above it. Now read your new sentence to yourself and decide which sentence is true.

This Is Giving Me a Headache.   When I do this exercise with my students, they usually write something such as "I have to do my homework" or "I have to go to school" or "I have to do a lot of chores." When I ask them to write *choose to* instead of *have to*, many of them argue at first.

"I don't choose to come to school," one boy insisted. "If my father didn't drive me here every day, I wouldn't ever come."

"Does your father hold your hand and walk you to class and sit down with you and stay all day long to make sure you're here?" I asked. Jeremiah rolled his eyes and said, "You know he doesn't."

"Well, then I guess you could just walk right out the back door, couldn't you?" I asked. "Look out the window. There are lots of kids cutting school. You could, too."

"No, I can't," Jeremiah said. "My dad would kill me when he found out."

"Oh," I said, "you don't want your dad to kill you, so you *choose* to come to school."

Jeremiah crossed his arms and refused to discuss the matter any further, but I could tell from his expression that he understood exactly what I was talking about. His second sentence was, "I can't pass algebra." When I instructed him to cross out *can't* and replace it with *don't want to*, Jeremiah hooted and clapped his hands.

"I got you, Miss J!" he yelled. "I never got a good grade in algebra in my life."

"Have you ever passed a math class?" I asked.

"Yeah, I passed pre-algebra last year," Jeremiah said, "but I can't pass this year."

"Have you gotten any answers correct on your homework in algebra?" I asked.

"I get some right, but I always get a D or F," Jeremiah said.

"And have you passed even one test this year?"

"I passed a couple, but I flunked more than I passed."

"Well, if you passed pre-algebra last year, and you passed some of the tests this year, that means there's nothing wrong with your brain. You can learn math," I said. "Don't you think there's anything in the whole universe that you could do to pass algebra this year?" Jeremiah shrugged. "What would you have to do?" I asked.

"I guess if I didn't do anything else but study math and got a tutor and did homework all night long, I could pass," he said.

"But you don't want to do all that, do you?" I asked. He shook his head. "Okay, then let's tell the truth. You don't want to pass algebra badly enough to do everything you would have to do to pass it. Am I right?" Jeremiah heaved a giant sigh and put his head down on his desk.

"This is giving me a headache," he mumbled into his arms.

"That's enough for now," I said. "But I want you to understand that there are very few things you cannot do in this world. And there are very few things you truly have to do. We have to eat, breathe, sleep, and go to the bathroom to stay alive. And we can't change our skin color or our families or our height. But other than that, we do things because we choose to and we don't do things because we don't really want to. So let's tell the truth to ourselves. That's the first step to becoming a truly powerful person. If you want to be successful in school, you can do it. If you fail, it's because you didn't want to be successful enough to work for it."

I think the reason that young people respond so well to this exercise is because it makes them feel powerful. Maybe you can still remember how hard it is to be young, to have adults decide what you should wear, eat, read, and do all day long, every single day. It's very difficult to accept so much direction. It makes children feel powerless. And it makes many of them frustrated and angry. The "Have to and Can't" exercise helps diffuse much of that frustration and anger, because it helps children realize that they do have control over much of their lives.

"You made the choice to walk into my classroom today," I often remind them. "And with that choice, that freedom, comes the responsibility to cooperate with me. That's what life is about. For every freedom you want to enjoy, for every choice you make, there are responsibilities that go along with the package."

Parents can make that same argument about any privilege. Responsibility is part of the package along with dating, driving, staying out late, and other privileges. In order to earn more independence and freedom, young people must show that they are responsible.

YOU CHOOSE WHO YOU ARE

Sometimes students will argue that their parents make them do things, that their lives are truly beyond control—and sometimes they are right. But I also remind them of this important idea: Even though adults may control much of your life, there is something that nobody can control, and that is your mind. Your attitude is your own personal choice. Every single second of every single day, you choose the way you are going to respond to your life. You can become angry, rebellious, or rude. Or you can choose to be cheerful, friendly, and polite to other people. Maybe you can't choose your skin color or how much money your family has or how you live at home, but you do choose whether or not you are a liar or an honest person, a quitter or a hard worker, a rude person or somebody who respects others. You choose the kind of person you are. You can choose to be a winner or a loser in life. Nobody can make you a failure, but you can make yourself a winner.

WHAT MAKES A GOOD SET OF RULES?

The rules of your house will be different from the rules at somebody else's house because your family is unique. But all good sets of rules have some things in common:

1. A good list of rules is short enough to remember easily.
2. Good rules are reasonable. They make sense.

3. Good rules are clear and specific—we know exactly what they mean.
4. Good rules make our lives safer, easier, or more enjoyable.

BE SPECIFIC OR YOU MAY BE SORRY

I used to think I had a good command of the English language, that I knew exactly what I wanted to say. But I realized I wasn't as articulate as I thought I was when one of my students kept interrupting my lessons to spit in the trash can. The first time it happened, I was too surprised to respond. In the middle of my presentation to the class, Bobby stood up, cleared his sinus cavities with a loud snort, walked across the room in front of me, and spit in the trash can. Then he quietly returned to his seat as though his behavior was perfectly normal. After class, I stopped him on the way out the door and asked him to be more polite in the future. The following day, the same sinus clearing and spitting activity took place in midpresentation. Again, I asked Bobby to be more polite. After the third episode, and the third request, he said, "How come you're picking on me? I'm being polite."

"You think it's polite to cough up a mouthful of phlegm and interrupt my lesson to walk across the room and spit in the trash can?"

"Yeah, it's polite," Bobby said. "I'm not spitting on the floor." He was serious. He assumed that my warning was for him to make sure he spit into the trash can and not on the floor near the can. When I explained that any bodily function that involved loud sounds or smells should be performed in the privacy of the bathroom, or at least outside behind a tree, Bobby nodded. After that day, I took care to make sure that my rules and requests were explicit and specific, so that my students would understand exactly what I expected. That example may sound ridiculous to you, but it's true. Children don't have the same frame of reference as adults do, so what seems obvious to us is often a mystery to them.

NOBODY WANTS TO BE THE BAD GUY

One of the hardest things about being the adult is that you have to be the "bad guy" sometimes. You have to be the party pooper, the one who brings us back to reality. But that's our job and if we don't do it, we can't expect our children to develop self-control and respect. Many times I have been tempted to be a friend instead of an adult, but I know that children need adult guidance more than they need friends who encourage them to act irresponsibly. For example, many of my students complain that they don't want to take biology or algebra or a foreign language. I tell them that I am sorry they are unhappy, but that it is my responsibility as an adult and as their parent or teacher to make sure that they are prepared for life after high school. I am willing for them to hate me for a while, in order to help them be better prepared.

"Maybe you don't plan to go to college now," I tell them, "and you may never go, but maybe you will change your mind later on. If that happens, you will be prepared. If it doesn't, then you will be well-educated. Either way, you will be better off than if I let you take easy classes now. It is my job to help you learn to make decisions, but I don't think you have the experience and knowledge to make the best decision on this matter right now. It has nothing to do with your intelligence. It has everything to do with me being a responsible adult and taking my job seriously. You are a precious and important person and I want to make sure I do the best job of helping you grow up to be the wonderful, successful person I know you can be." (It may sound hokey to you, but it won't sound hokey to them. Trust me.)

THE LETTER OF THE LAW

The most important part of rule making is not making rules or enforcing them. The most important step is assigning consequences for the people who break your rules. If the consequences are reasonable, fair, and consistently applied, people will accept your authority and follow your rules. They will respect you for doing your job. If you punish one person and not another or assign different consequences to different people for breaking the same rule, you may end up with a mutiny on your hands.

Some people prefer the democratic method, including their children's input into the making of household rules. If it works for you, that's fine. I'm not very democratic in the classroom or at home. In the classroom, I stand behind my two basic rules because I think they are good and reasonable rules. At home, my husband and I are the rule-making team. Then we pass the word to my stepchildren. If they protest, my husband and I hold a private conference and decide whether to change a rule. The final answer is our decision and we make that clear to the children. Their safety and well-being are our responsibility, so we must make the rules that we believe will be best for them.

CONSEQUENCES VERSUS PUNISHMENT

It took me a while to learn to assign consequences instead of punishments for children who are irresponsible or not motivated to succeed in school. When I first began teaching, my master teacher advised me not to use writing assignments as punishment. "You don't want the kids to associate writing with feeling angry or guilty," he said, "otherwise, they'll start to hate writing. Make the punishment fit the crime. If a kid forgets to bring an important book, make him carry fifteen books around for a week. Making him write an essay has nothing to do with what he did wrong. You won't be teaching him responsibility—you'll be teaching him to hate writing."

It's difficult, sometimes, to think of meaningful consequences for children's misbehavior, but I believe my master teacher was right. The consequences should teach something, if at all possible. If a teenager fails to return the family car at the specified time, for example, taking away television privileges wouldn't address the problem.

Taking away the teenager's driving privileges for a week or two would be much more effective.

Speaking of suspending TV privileges—I recently read an editorial column in a newspaper wherein the author said she wanted her daughter to stop watching so much TV. She wanted her to participate in something that required more intellectual challenge or physical activity. But when the author really wanted to punish her daughter, she took away her daughter's TV watching privileges. No TV for a week was the ultimate punishment at their house. Then the author realized she was defeating her own purpose—she was making TV even more important to her daughter because the message she was sending was, "If I really want to hurt you, I take away the most important thing, the television." I hadn't thought about it in that way, but the author of that column makes a very good point. We do teach children what is valuable and important by either giving it to them as a reward or denying it to them as punishment. Perhaps we should reward children's good behavior by allowing them time to read, and punish them by making them watch TV! Something tells me that plan needs a little work, but I think it has potential.

STICK TO THE POINT

My mother was good at assigning consequences to teach responsibility, although I didn't realize it as a child. When I was four years old, I walked two blocks down the street to the neighborhood grocery store with my mother. I didn't understand that we had to pay for our food. I thought we went to the store, walked around, said hello to Edna, the cashier, and went home with our treasures. That day, I picked up a large package of bubble gum and carried it home. When my mother asked where I got the gum, I told her I got it at the store. She didn't spank me or yell at me. Instead, she explained that we must pay for everything we take from the store or else we are stealing. Then she made me take all the money out of my piggy bank and walk back to the store by myself. I had to give the money to Mr. Winston, the manager, and tell him I was sorry I stole gum from his store. Then I had to give back the gum, too! Nobody told me I was a bad girl, but I felt terrible, and the consequences my mother assigned were much more effective than a spanking or other punishment would have been. In all of my life, I have never stolen another thing.

I'm not as good as my mother was at handling misbehavior calmly and logically. Perhaps you have no problem enforcing rules. Perhaps you calmly assess the situation and assign the proper consequences, without becoming upset or critical. But if you're anything like me, you hate to hurt anybody's feelings, and it hurts your feelings when people become angry with you, even little people. So, sometimes I become too indulgent and give a weak response when children break rules that I have set for them. Instead of holding them responsible for their behavior, I try to make the incident go away. At other times, I become so frustrated that I criticize the student instead of trying to solve the problem at hand. For example, a student comes to class without her homework and explains that she forgot what I had assigned. If she is a good student, I might say, "That's okay.

You usually turn in all your work. One assignment won't hurt your grade. Just don't let it happen again." If she is a poor student, one who frequently forgets her work, I might say, "Again? You're always forgetting your homework. Can't you remember anything?"

Neither of those responses helps the student learn from the situation. In the first example, I am telling the good student that she can get away with acting irresponsibly once in a while. In the second example, I'm telling the student that she has a character flaw. She might even interpret my response to mean that I don't think she is smart enough to remember her assignments.

I need to stick to the point in handling this situation. The issue in this case is the forgotten homework, not whether the student holds a high or low grade in my class. My response for either student should be, "I'm sorry you forgot your homework, but it's important for you to remember your work or your grades will suffer. Homework is your responsibility. If you forget an assignment, call someone and find out what you are supposed to do." With that response, I haven't criticized the student or made her feel ashamed, but I have reminded her that she is responsible for her work, and I have provided a suggestion for future behavior.

Let's look at another example, one that might happen at your home. A child drops a glass and spills fruit juice on the floor. You could respond with criticism: "Why can't you be more careful? Haven't I told you not to try to pour the juice yourself?" Or you could nurture the child: "Don't cry. It's just juice. Let me clean it up for you." We still haven't addressed the issue of juice on the floor and how to avoid making the same mistake. A better response would be, "I know you didn't mean to spill the juice, but everybody makes mistakes. You must remember to ask me for help when you want to pour the juice because the bottle is very heavy. You need to clean up this mess and then I will help you pour another glass." Now you are reminding the child that nobody is perfect, but that we need to correct our mistakes.

It's difficult, sometimes, to think of the right thing to say, especially in a crisis. And, unfortunately, some of us were raised by parents who criticized us every time we did anything wrong or used spanking as their only disciplinary tool. We learn to parent from our parents, so we tend to do the same things they did. It takes a conscious effort to change our behavior and learn to respond differently. With practice, however, it becomes easier to remember to address the problem and not attack or protect the child who made the mistake. You may even find yourself treating yourself differently. When you make a mistake, instead of just waving your hands in the air and saying, "Oh, well, those things happen" or "How could I be so stupid? Why can't I do anything right?" you may begin to look at your behavior more objectively. You may remind yourself that nobody's perfect, to learn from your mistakes, and to think of ways to avoid making the same errors in the future.

RESPONSIBILITY IS A WINNER

It isn't surprising that students who have responsibilities at home do better in school. That's simple common sense—it's no wonder that research studies back up the idea. What kind of responsibilities should you assign? That will depend upon your child's maturity and your own personality. My mother, for example, preferred to do all of the cooking for seven people rather than clean up after us as we learned to cook, so we weren't given responsibilities that included cooking. My Grandma Johnson didn't believe anybody else could wash the dishes as well as she could. Even if somebody else washed them, she washed them again. Perhaps you are the sole cook and bottle washer in your home. Fine. Cooking and washing dishes aren't the only things children can do. There are plenty of other responsibilities that you can assign to your child.

Even small children can participate in running a household. A four-year-old may not be able to take out the trash or feed the pets, but she can put a new liner bag in the trash can or pour a glass of water into the dog's dish. One child can be responsible for collecting the mail from the mailbox each day or for mailing any letters that need to go out. What we consider tiresome chores can be exciting challenges to kids, and they don't mind repetition. Many kids can be convinced that vacuuming is fun. One of my stepsons thinks it's a treat to be allowed to help wash dishes. My sister used to beg to be allowed to mop the kitchen floor. If we don't tell children that housework is a bore, some of them will think it's wonderful fun.

The more children are allowed to participate as a family member, the stronger sense of responsibility they will have in making sure that the household runs smoothly. They will view themselves as valuable members of the family, and that will become more important as they enter their adolescence and peer pressure is at its peak. The stronger your family ties, the more equipped your child will be to resist temptations.

SAVE THE BABY-SITTERS

On behalf of all the children who are expected to baby-sit for younger brothers and sisters, I'd like to ask you to consider what a large responsibility child care is. Perhaps you have a good reason for asking your child to baby-sit frequently—you can't afford to hire an outside person, or you don't feel comfortable leaving your children with strangers or non–family members. But please treat your child with the same respect and courtesy you would offer to a person you had hired. Try to arrange to give her free time whenever you can, so she has a chance to be carefree for at least some time during the day. Make sure she knows you appreciate her time and effort, and try to compensate her fairly. If you don't have the money to pay your child the standard rate for child care, then try to compensate in some other way—by giving her special privileges or extra attention. We need to treat our children as we would want to be treated. It sounds clichéd and simplistic, but it's something we need to remember. Children are short people, but it doesn't mean they don't have feelings or logic or the right to be treated with dignity and respect.

PUNISHMENTS VERSUS REWARDS

Punishments and rewards work in the same way as positive and negative rules do. Positive rules encourage good behavior much more effectively than negative rules prevent bad behavior. Rewarding children for acting the way we want them to act is much more effective than punishing them for misbehaving. Think back to your own childhood. Can you remember how you felt when you were punished? Did it make you change your attitude and behavior immediately? Or did it make you feel ashamed, humiliated, powerless, and angry? Usually, punishment creates anger and, quite often, a desire for revenge. I can remember sitting in my room, my bottom stinging from a hard spanking, thinking of ways to get even with my father. On that particular day, I had been spanked for forgetting to help my sister clean off the dinner dishes and load them into the dishwasher. The spanking didn't inspire me to rush down and wash dishes. Instead, I sneaked downstairs during the night and used a sharp paring knife to cut little slashes in the rubber seal all the way around the top of the dishwasher. After that, it leaked, and I got another spanking. And the cycle continued.

A similar cycle started when I began teaching. One of my first assignments was as student teacher for a class of college-bound high school sophomores. They were perfect angels until my master teacher left me in charge; then they became uncontrollable little stinkers. They didn't dislike me personally—they didn't even know me. They just didn't feel like cooperating with me. (Later, one of the girls in that class told me they wanted to see if they could make me have a nervous breakdown, so they could see if

I would really foam at the mouth.) From that first day, they refused to be quiet and let me talk to them. They ignored me and chatted with each other for the entire class period. The following day, I assigned seats instead of letting them choose their own. The more they argued, the more I insisted. I thought I had won the war when they all sat in their assigned seats. The next day, they tried a different approach. Whenever I turned my back to write on the board or find a book, they all dropped their books flat on the floor. It made a horrible noise and it also made me angry, but I didn't want to send them to the office or call in my master teacher for help. I wanted to prove that I could handle the situation. After all, they were only children, I thought. What I didn't realize then was that children don't have jobs and families to raise; they can devote all of their time and energy to getting even with an adult who punishes them.

Every day the tension built higher. After three weeks, we were at a total standstill. They sat in their assigned seats and they did their work because they knew they would fail if they didn't, but they did nothing they didn't have to do. If I asked a question and somebody tried to answer, the other students would all cough loudly, drowning out the would-be speaker. Finally, I realized I couldn't fix the problem. I called in my master teacher to observe the class. The students behaved a little better when he was in the room, but they still made my life miserable. After class, Hal Gray sat in one of the student desks and raised his hand. "Miss Johnson, you don't like us."

"You didn't like me first," I said.

"That's not the point," Hal said. "You're the adult.

You're supposed to be teaching them how to act. What you're teaching them now is how to be a bully."

I protested my innocence. It was their fault in the first place, I insisted, because they refused to cooperate with me.

"Then why don't you figure out how to get them to cooperate," Hal asked, "instead of trying to get even with them or control them?"

For a long time that evening, I muttered around my house, insulted that Hal didn't support me. I was trying my hardest, but they simply wouldn't cooperate. Finally, I decided I had nothing else to lose, so I tried to think of some way to do what Hal suggested. I tried to remember what my own teachers had done to make me cooperate with them. The next day, I announced to the class that I wanted to apologize for being mean to them. I told them they had put me on the defensive the first day and that they had hurt my feelings and made me angry. I said I wanted to start over and try being nice to each other, if they would agree to cooperate. A few students looked interested, but most of them just sat and looked at me, trying to figure out whether it was a trick. They didn't behave perfectly that day, but they didn't seem as motivated to misbehave either. They were confused. I hadn't reacted as they expected me to. They wanted me to fight with them. If I refused to fight, it wasn't any fun.

That night, I wrote notes to the parents of a few of the students in that class. The following day, I gave the notes to the students and asked them to deliver them to their parents. Of course, they expected the notes to be complaints about them. Imagine one girl's surprise when she peeked at the note, which I expected, and read, "I just wanted to tell you how much I enjoy having Callie in my class. She is very bright and has a great sense of humor. It's a pleasure to be her teacher." I knew Jason read his note because he blushed and stared at his desk for most of the class period. Jason was one of the worst students in class, the leader of the pack, and he seemed to enjoy tormenting me. On his note, I had written, "Jason is one of the brightest young men I have ever had the pleasure of teaching. He is very charming and has excellent leadership skills."

Within a few days, half of the students had decided to cooperate with me, and the others gave up the fight. It was an important lesson to me and one I have never forgotten. *I can control the environment, but I cannot control the child.* I can threaten and bribe and punish, but I can't make students do something they don't want to do. So, I am better off trying to motivate them to behave, rewarding them for doing what I want them to do. It's much more effective than trying to make them do things and punishing them when they don't.

LOOK FOR EXCUSES TO PRAISE

I'm sure you've felt, at one time or another, that your supervisor at work, or the people in your family, never notice when you do something well. But they certainly notice when you make a mistake. Children often feel that way, and quite often they are right. We spend far more time criticizing and correcting them than we do praising and rewarding them. Instead of trying to catch them being bad, we need to try to catch them being good.

When the report card arrives, compliment your child on the good grades. (If there are *no* good grades, you have a serious motivation problem or learning disability on your hands.) Of course, say that you'd like to see those other grades improve, but concentrate on the highest grades and tell your child how proud you are of those passing grades.

When your child completes a homework assignment, ask to see it. Find something good about it: accuracy, completeness, neat handwriting, creativity, artistic flair.

When your child tells about somebody who misbehaved at school, ask your child whether he or she also misbehaved. If not, praise your child for behaving well and setting a good example. Tell him you are proud that he didn't let other children influence him to behave badly.

Try to catch children doing well at home, too. If they make their beds without being asked, thank them. Shake their hands. It works. It works especially well when there are two or more children in the family. Children love attention. Some of them even prefer negative attention to none at all. If they don't believe they can earn positive attention, some will go out of their way to cause trouble, hoping you'll notice.

USE POSITIVE PEER PRESSURE

When I had an entire class filled with students who "forgot" to do their homework, I tried threatening them with bad grades, but they already had bad grades, so it didn't work. I tried giving motivational speeches at the end of class. Still no homework. Finally, I decided to give all of my attention to the few students in that class who did do their work. I worried that the other students would resent them, but I decided to take a chance. I put Snoopy and Garfield stickers on the papers of the students who did their homework, even if they had several incorrect answers. I thanked them, in front of the other students, for making the effort. I also shook their hands, one at a time, when I returned the papers. These were high school students. They were too cool for "baby tricks" like stickers. Or so they said. But within a month, every student in that class was turning in enough homework to earn a passing grade!

I tried the same thing at home, with my four stepchildren. Only Brian, the youngest at age five, made his bed in the morning. The others always conveniently forgot. I tried reminding them to make their beds, and thanking them afterward, but I wanted them to do it themselves. So, I started shaking Brian's hand, thanking him, giving him a big hug and a kiss, and telling him how proud I was. I expected the older children to gang up on Brian, call him a "brownie," and try to persuade him to stop making them look bad. They didn't. Eric, age nine, was the first to join Brian. After just a few days of sitting at the breakfast table, watching Brian receive handshakes and hugs, Eric announced one morning that his bed was made if I'd like to go and see for myself. Within a week, Sean and Brigit, ages twelve and fourteen, had joined the little bed makers. They grinned self-consciously when I hugged them, and pretended they hadn't done it for the praise. They acted as if making their beds had been their idea the whole time, that they had just forgotten for a while. I didn't spoil their fantasy.

BE PREPARED

If you haven't made a habit of compliments, your children may go into shock temporarily when you start thanking them and praising them. They are prepared for criticism and punishments, but they sometimes don't know how to act when people hand them compliments. They may roll their eyes and shake their heads, or run out of the room, or pretend they don't care, or announce that they see right through your child psychology. When a student accuses me of trying to use child psychology on her, I always say, "Oh, no. I'd never try that on you. I know you're too smart to fall for something so obvious." Then I keep right on using that same child psychology and it usually works.

WHY BOTHER?

One parent asked me why he should reward his daughter for doing what she was supposed to do in the first place. "I feel like I'm bribing her or something," he said. "She's supposed to behave. Why should I thank her for doing what she should do?"

There's a very simple—and true—answer to that question. If we don't reward children for behaving, what will motivate them to continue? I can't tell you how many students I have had whose parents have remarked that their son or daughter "used to be such a good student."

"I just don't know what happened to Jose," one mother confided. "He had straight A's until eighth grade, and now look at him. B's and C's and sometimes a D. He's so smart, but he just won't try. I think it must be his friends. He hangs out with the wrong crowd."

Jose and I had a good rapport, so I asked him why he had stopped earning straight A's. I didn't tell him what his mother had said. I wanted to hear his opinion. I expected him to shrug, or say high school was hard, or that he didn't care about it. He surprised me.

"I was a good little kid," Jose said. "I even had all A's on my report card when I was little. But one day I looked around and I realized nobody cared. Nobody really respected me for doing all that work, so I stopped doing it. Now I don't get such good grades, but I get a lot more respect from people."

I think what Jose considered respect was simple attention. Parents, teachers, and school counselors tend to focus on the students who are causing trouble or having problems in school. We need to focus as much attention on those students who are succeeding. For many children, good grades aren't enough by themselves. If we don't recognize and reward them for their good behavior, they lose their desire and motivation to succeed.

RECOGNITION IS FREE, SIMPLE, AND NONFATTENING

Recognition doesn't have to be elaborate, but it does need to be immediate, sincere, and frequent. It doesn't work to make up things or give praise just to say the words. And it's important to catch children in the act of behaving just as we catch them misbehaving. Both con-

sequences for breaking rules and recognition for following them need to be immediate. It's the same concept as
house training a puppy. It does no good to spank a
puppy and put it outside an hour after it has piddled on
the kitchen floor. It doesn't make the connection between its behavior and its punishment. Likewise, if a
puppy goes to the bathroom outdoors, it won't make the
connection if you wait fifteen minutes until after the
deed is done to pat it on the head.

If you have a hard time seeing your child's good behavior, here are some things to look for (and if you're a
little tongue-tied, I've offered some suggestions for what
to say—praise works best when you phrase it so that it's
personal):

- siblings who spend time in the same room without
  squabbling (Thanks for being nice.)
- doing homework early or without being prompted
  (You're being very responsible.)
- putting dirty clothes in the hamper without being asked
  (Thanks for helping out.)
- leaving the bathroom neat and clean after a bath or
  shower (You are very considerate.)
- helping another child complete a difficult task (You're
  a thoughtful, kind person.)
- listening politely to an elderly neighbor's story (You're
  a kind, considerate person.)
- opening the door for somebody else at a store (That was
  very thoughtful of you.)
- using good manners at a restaurant (Your good manners
  make me feel proud of you.)

- working hard to finish something or taking time to correct an error (Good for you.)
- demonstrating creativity in music, art, or writing (You're very creative.)
- being patient or spending time with a young child (You're acting very grown-up.)
- sharing an idea or opinion with you (Thanks for sharing your thoughts with me.)

Again, if you aren't used to giving praise, it may feel or sound funny to you when you first say these things, but I promise you that children won't think you sound funny at all. They may blush and tell you to be quiet, but I promise you that they don't mean it.

REWARDS

Rewards, unlike recognition, should be infrequent and long-term. A reward at the end of a week is enough for young children. For older children, the promise of a big reward in one or two, even three, years can be very effective. Many parents have had great success by offering a stereo, a computer, or a car at the end of the school year, or upon graduation from high school or college. The father of one of my students decided that desperate measures were required when his son was sixteen and failing half of his courses. Mr. Dexter bought a decent used car, painted it bright red, waxed it, and parked it in the driveway. When Darrell came home from school and saw the car, his father said, "If you pass every class this semester and get a part-time job to pay for your insurance, that car is yours." It worked. Darrell's grades went up, he got a job, and still had the job and the car two years later when he graduated with his class.

Another student, Tony, was a sophomore who wanted to be a jet pilot. Tony spent every spare minute sketching different aircraft in the margins of his papers and on the covers of his notebooks. Unfortunately, because of his grades, Tony had little chance of becoming a pilot. If he didn't make some major changes, he wouldn't make it past the tenth grade. Repeated parent-teacher conferences didn't work—he always promised to do better, but just couldn't maintain the effort on his own.

That year, I received an unexpected tax return. It wasn't a large sum of money, but it was enough to buy two discount round-trip plane tickets from San Francisco to San Diego. I asked Tony's parents if I could offer him a trip at the end of the year if he passed every class. They agreed. When I told Tony about my plan, he didn't respond as I had expected. He didn't even smile. He just looked at me for a minute, then nodded his head. I wondered whether he thought I was teasing him, or whether his talk about becoming a pilot was just talk. He didn't seem excited, but his grades did improve over the following weeks and he passed all of his classes.

As a journalist in the navy, I had been stationed at North Island Naval Air Station on Coronado Island in San Diego. I called the public affairs officer at Fleet Aviation Support Operational Training Group (FASOTRA-GRUPAC) and asked whether it might be possible for Tony to tour one of the hangars on base and see some different aircraft. The navy did much better than that. Not only did we get a tour of the hangar, Tony had the chance to fly the plane in one of the flight simulators used to train pilots. He landed a fighter on an aircraft carrier at night—something a lot of adult pilots find difficult! For the first time, Tony acted excited about something. He beamed as the training crew patted him on the back and gave him a "thumbs up."

When we returned the following day, I told Tony, "Now you know that you can fly a plane. And you have proved that you can pass all your classes. Do the same things every year that you did this year and you will be a success." Unfortunately, I transferred to another school the following year, so I wasn't there to see it, but Tony did graduate on time with his class two years later. I don't know whether he'll become a pilot, but I don't regret spending the time or money to support his dream.

Perhaps you can't afford something as expensive as a car or a plane trip or don't believe in spending so much money on rewards. There are plenty of less expensive rewards you can offer your child. In fact, some of the best rewards are free: a weekend with no household chores, an afternoon roaming the mall, a trip to a large public or university library, permission to stay up late and watch a movie on TV, a sleep-over with friends, a day of fishing or hiking, a day trip to the mountains or seashore. The rewards you choose will depend on your income, your personality, and your relationship with your child. What's important is to make the reward something your child will truly enjoy, not something you want to do or something you think your child *should* enjoy.

RANDOM REWARDS

Do you remember when your teachers gave pop quizzes as an incentive to studying? The more you studied, the better chance you had of passing those pop quizzes. Not all students respond to the threat of pop quizzes by studying more, but many do. The same principle works with rewards. By accident, I discovered that my students turned in a lot more homework assignments when I randomly rewarded the students who did their homework, instead of punishing those who didn't. So I started the Homework Lottery. When I collected homework papers, I wrote the date and the name of each student who did the work on slips of paper and popped them into a big glass jar on my desk. Once or twice a week, I would stop in the middle of class, pull a name from the jar, and give the winner a prize. Lottery prizes weren't expensive. One day, the winner might receive a piece of bubble gum or a certificate worth five points on the next exam. Another day, the prize might be a disposable camera or a videotape of a popular movie. In many cases, the students seemed to care more about being a winner than they did about receiving a prize. After a few weeks of running my lottery, I had an 85 percent homework rate in all of my classes.

A variation of the Homework Lottery could be used at home, to reward children for completing schoolwork or household chores. Because they never know when the reward will be given, children will figure out that they can increase their chances of winning by doing their homework and chores more often.

BRIBERY ISN'T A DIRTY WORD

People have accused me of bribing my students to succeed. My response is "If my choice is between threatening and punishing them if they fail, or bribing them to succeed, I prefer to bribe them. I don't mind bribing students to achieve success because once they have succeeded, they will want that feeling of satisfaction again, and I won't have to bribe them again." It's true. Once a child knows how good it feels to succeed, he or she will work to achieve that feeling again. Unfortunately, many children need motivation to achieve that first success or to establish good patterns of behavior. We don't seem to have any problem criticizing and punishing them for misbehavior, so why not spend as much time and energy praising and rewarding them for behaving well? As always, I try to view my students as employees. I ask myself what would motivate me more—a boss who came to work on Monday and said, "If you don't do what I tell you to do this week, I will fire you on Friday," or a boss who said, "I have a lot of hard work for you this week, but if you do it well, I will give you a big check and perhaps a bonus on Friday." No contest.

Chapter 6

THE THREE R'S: READ, READ, READ

❖

READING IS REALLY FUNDAMENTAL

Reading is the most important skill required for success in school. Good readers tend to earn good grades. Poor readers suffer in math because they don't understand the problems; they suffer in science classes because they don't understand the instructions for experiments; they suffer in history and biology because they can't keep up with the volume of reading required in those subjects; they suffer in English because they can't answer questions or write essays about literature that they don't understand. I'm not talking about speed reading. Faster isn't necessarily better, although slow readers often panic or give up because it takes them so long to complete an assignment. I'm talking about comprehension, understanding what's on the page. You would be surprised how many students *seem* to read well, with good diction and pronunciation, but have no idea what they're reading.

COMPREHENSION IS THE KEY

When I realized that one of my tenth-graders couldn't answer the simplest questions based on any of his reading assignments, I was appalled. How could teachers have passed this student for ten years of school? I wondered. Surely, one of those teachers would have had the ethics and empathy to address his problem. I asked Leroy to come and visit me at lunchtime. When he arrived, I asked him whether he had always had problems reading.

"I don't have a problem," Leroy insisted. "I can read really good." He picked up a book and read a couple of paragraphs. He was right. He could read. He pronounced the words correctly and paused where punctuation marks indicated a pause. But when I asked Leroy to briefly summarize, in his own words, what he had just read, he shrugged his shoulders. "I don't remember," he said. "I can never remember. I used to think I was dumb or something, but that only happens when I read by myself. When other kids read out loud in class, I remember everything."

He was right again. During class discussions of stories and poems, Leroy always had something intelligent to add and he clearly understood the reading. And I understood how he had managed to get to the tenth grade. Because his reading skills were poor, he had learned to be an excellent listener and to memorize more quickly than most people do. He earned high enough grades on other assignments—vocabulary, spelling, personal essays— to balance the poor grades he earned on reading comprehension. His other teachers must have assumed that he simply didn't try very hard on the reading. And if they had suspected a problem and asked Leroy to read out loud, they would have been satisfied that he could read. That's one of the problems with overcrowded classrooms. When there are thirty-five or forty students in a class, teachers don't have the time and energy required to address every individual student's needs. And that's where parents and guardians come in. If you can figure out what your child needs, you can get help from teachers, counselors, or special tutors. (I know, I know— it's the school's job and not yours to teach your child, but if the school isn't doing it, and you refuse to do it because it isn't your job, your child is the one who suffers. We all need to do what we can.)

After hearing Leroy "read," I asked him, "What happens when you have to read by yourself and answer questions?" I still couldn't quite understand what was happening in his brain. How could he read so well and yet read so poorly?

"I can't remember the stuff," Leroy said, "and then I get mad because I feel dumb."

"You aren't dumb," I assured him, "but there seems to be a problem. If we can figure it out, maybe we can fix it. I need to know what happens when you read."

"The words just go right through my head," Leroy said.

He moved one finger in front of his face, quickly, from right to left. "There it is, then it's gone."

I asked him whether it was like reading one of those neon signs like they have in front of the bank that tell the temperature and time. Or the messages that sometimes run across the bottom of the television screen, letting viewers know the score of a big game, or what's happening on the latest news stories.

"Yeah," Leroy said, "it's just like that. I only remember the words when they're right in front of me. As soon as they leave, they're gone."

As it turned out, Leroy had been taught to read phonetically and had learned his grammar lessons so he knew that a comma indicated a short pause and a period a longer one. But he hadn't learned reading comprehension. He didn't realize that he was supposed to concentrate on what he was reading, to understand the meaning. He thought reading consisted of pronouncing the words correctly. Once we identified the problem, it didn't go away immediately. I'm not a reading teacher, and I haven't been formally trained to teach reading, but I did make an appointment for Leroy to meet with a counselor. When we explained the situation, Leroy was placed in a remedial reading class with a teacher who was trained to help students overcome reading problems. His progress was slow at first, but eventually he learned how to read well. The biggest factor in his success was understanding the problem and realizing that it had nothing to do with his intelligence. He had never asked for help because he thought his teachers would think he was stupid.

IS THERE A PROBLEM?

The first clue that your child has a reading problem is if he hates to read. It's human nature not to like the things we do poorly. It may be a simple matter of practice. The more a child reads, the easier it gets. At some point, after enough practice, the child will become such an accomplished reader that he will forget he's reading. He'll be entertained or educated or provoked to think by the words on the page, without straining to read.

How long it takes to learn to read well is an individual matter. It's like dancing. Some people have to practice the same steps over and over before they can waltz without counting, "One, two, three" under their breaths. Other people practice the same steps for just a few minutes before they begin whirling around the dance floor. Once I was taking a group dance lesson and one of the other dance students told me that the instructor used to be one of the worst dancers she had ever seen. "I swear he had two left feet," the woman said. "But he wanted to be a dance instructor. So he practiced every day for hours and look at him now. He's not Fred Astaire, but he's a pretty good dancer—and he gets paid to dance."

One child may take a week to learn to read, while another child needs several months. The first child is not necessarily more intelligent. He or she may simply have more natural ability for that particular task. The child who learns to read more slowly may end up having better comprehension skills later on.

What if your child refuses to read at all? She may be too young and simply not ready to read yet. Or she may be exercising her willpower. In that case, I'd forget about reading until the child indicates an interest. I think age grouping is one of the biggest problems in our educational system. Every child has his or her own time line for development, and it may not fit the pattern dictated by the school curriculum. When that happens, instead of making adjustments to meet the child's need, the child is expected to speed up or slow down to meet the needs of the school. In one sophomore class, I had several boys, all fifteen years old. One boy was taller than me and had a full beard and mustache. Some of the other boys had a little "peach fuzz," and a few still had their baby fat and were much shorter than the others. My question is this: Given the marked differences in those boys' physical development, why in the world would we expect them to be at the same stage of mental development?

Most children reach an age where they want to read because they want to do what the "big kids" do. If your child doesn't read until third grade, don't focus on the fact that his brother read at age three or that the neighbor children all learned in kindergarten. Instead, make sure that your child doesn't have a vision or hearing problem and that he hasn't been absent from school during the time when basic reading skills were being taught.

If your child has trouble reading, and you are certain that the trouble is not caused by immaturity, lack of practice, or inadequate instruction, then your first step should be an eye exam. Many school health offices can give simple vision exams. You might also consider hearing problems— some children have trouble following the reading teacher's instructions because they don't hear well. Light sensitivity might also be a contributing factor (see pages 41–47). Learning disabilities such as dyslexia can also cause problems with reading. We'll discuss learning disabilities in Chapter 9.

IS YOUR CHILD REALLY READING?

Comprehension is important, even for young children who are just beginning to read. Without comprehension, children will read the "neon sign," as Leroy did, and not understand a word of what they've read. You can help your child develop better comprehension skills by asking him to read out loud to you, then asking questions. Start with simple questions: What was the character's name? What color are his eyes? Then, ask some questions that require thinking: Why did the character act in a certain way? What else could she have done? What do you think will happen next in this story?

Regardless of the age of your child and the difficulty of the reading material, you can ask questions to help improve reading comprehension. (And you don't have to have read the book in question, or understand it. Don't worry if you don't remember Shakespeare. You can still ask intelligent questions that will provoke good thinking.) If you need some help getting started, here is a brief list of questions that you might ask your child about different school assignments.

Reading a novel, play, or short story:

1. Who is the main character in this story?
2. What does this character look like? How does he or she act?

3. Do you like this character? Why or why not?
4. Pick two characters and tell how they are the same and how they are different. Which one would you rather be? Why?
5. Is this a good story? Why or why not?

Reading nonfiction—newspaper or magazine articles and editorials:

1. What is the most important idea in this article? Why did you select that particular idea as most important?
2. What kind of support does the author use to convince you that this idea is correct or sound? Do you think the support is reliable? Do you believe it?
3. Did the author explain this idea well? Why or why not?
4. What will you remember most from this article?
5. If this is a controversial issue, does the author take sides? Do you agree or disagree with the author and why?

Reading a history textbook:

1. What are the main events in this chapter?
2. Why are those events important? Why do you think they're in the book?
3. How did those events affect the country (or the world)?
4. Do you think the same thing(s) could happen today? Why or why not?

5. If they did happen, what do you think would be the result?
6. If you were in charge of the country, what action would you take to prevent (if the events are negative) or cause (if events are positive) these things to happen here?

Reading a science or math textbook:

1. Explain in your own words the concept or process involved in this chapter.
2. In order to understand this concept, what did you have to remember that you already learned?
3. Why do you think scientists or mathematicians came up with this theory or concept?
4. Is this a good or valid theory? Why or why not?
5. Can you think of your own theory or experiment?
6. Why do you think this particular experiment, theory, or idea is included in the textbook? (Ask your teacher the following day and see whether you came up with the same reasons.)

GOOD READERS TEND TO BE GOOD THINKERS

You may have heard the term "higher level critical thinking skills." It's a popular concept in education reform, and it is important because critical thinking skills are what we use every day in solving life's problems. I think that if you understand the different levels of thinking, you will be better able to help your child develop good thinking skills. Most psychology students and many teachers in training study Benjamin Bloom's Taxonomy of Cognitive Domains, which is a fancy way of listing six different levels of thinking, from easiest to hardest. I teach the taxonomy to my students because I want them to understand why I assign a particular task in my class. I want them to be aware of how they are thinking and how to improve their thinking.

BLOOM'S TAXONOMY OF COGNITIVE DOMAINS

Bloom believed that people use six levels of thinking, each a little more complicated than the previous one. The six levels are: recall, comprehension, application, analysis, synthesis, and evaluation. The following discussion defines each level and gives examples of tasks that might be assigned to students.

RECALL – **remembering information.** Simple tasks such as reciting the alphabet, listing the different colors in the rainbow, recognizing shapes such as squares or circles, saying the definition of the words *fact* and *opinion.*

COMPREHENSION – **understanding things.** Understanding that words are made up of letters, that green is made of blue and yellow, that a square has four equal sides, that a fact is true and an opinion is what somebody thinks.

APPLICATION – using things you understand. Reading or writing words, finding the verb in a sentence, creating green paint by mixing blue and yellow, drawing a square or a circle, identifying a statement as either fact or opinion.

ANALYZING – comparing different things. Underlining all the verbs in a paragraph, then circling all the active verbs, explaining why a particular sentence is a fact or an opinion, finding the only square in a group of rectangles.

SYNTHESIS – making your own examples or materials. Making up your own sentences that contain action verbs. Writing a paragraph that states your own opinion. Composing a factual report based on your research and reading.

EVALUATION – making judgments based on your knowledge. Deciding which of three different action verbs (*pitching*, *tossing*, *hurling*) best describes the act of throwing a ball; reading two different opinions on the same subject and deciding which is better by giving specific examples to support your decision.

Critical thinking skills aren't restricted to school assignments. We use those same levels of thinking in our personal lives. When I present Bloom's theory to my students in school, I also give them a chart that shows how those same six levels of thinking might apply to their personal lives. The better we think, the better equipped we are to make decisions and solve the problems that arise in our daily lives. When students realize that there is a reason for the things we ask them to do, even if the reason isn't obvious at the time, they are much more inclined to cooperate.

Using Bloom's Taxonomy in Your Real Life

RECALL – Remembering all the words to a song or all the foods on your grocery list; reciting the stats of your favorite baseball team; listing all the parts of an engine or a stereo system.

COMPREHENSION – Understanding the difference between a receiver and an amplifier; knowing how a gasoline engine or computer works; realizing that some people are shy.

APPLICATION – Installing a stereo or changing the spark plugs in your car; making your own guacamole; filling out a job application with proper grammar; making friends with a shy person; fixing a toaster without electrocuting yourself.

ANALYZING – Deciding which job to accept; picking the best college for you; deciding whether to get married now, whether to open a credit card account, whether to send your kids to private school, join a gang, quit smoking, start using drugs, do your homework . . .

SYNTHESIS – Making a plan for your life and putting it into action; creating your own heavy metal band; starting your own business; building a house; making a budget based on your monthly income; raising healthy children.

EVALUATION – Deciding whether your current job offers the kind of future you want; reading the news and deciding whether it was presented truthfully; figuring out the best way to discipline your kids; deciding what will be best for your children if your spouse asks for a divorce; figuring out what went wrong and how to make things work better.

USING BLOOM'S TAXONOMY AT HOME

Keeping those six levels of thinking in mind, you can help your children develop and practice good thinking skills in their daily lives, as well as working on school assignments. Unless you are very unusual, most of your family conversations won't center on homework or school subjects. You can still practice critical thinking skills in your conversation. On laundry day, you might ask a young child, "Why do you think we put the white clothes in one pile and the bright colors into another? What would happen if we put them all together? Would it make a difference if we used hot or cold water? Why?" At dinnertime, ask your child to figure out starting times for three different foods (pork chops, rice, and peas, for example) that you want to be ready to eat at the same time. Which one will have to be started first? Which next?

When you stop for gas, ask your child to figure out how much you will save if you buy regular unleaded versus premium. Then ask whether she thinks it would be a good investment of your money to buy the premium. Why or why not? If she doesn't know the difference between regular and premium (I'm not sure I know myself), ask her where she thinks you could find out that information.

Evaluation is the highest level thinking skill, but children tend to view it as the easiest. After all, it isn't difficult to give an opinion or choose the better of two videos to rent. But, as we all know, it's easy to make poor choices and jump to incorrect conclusions. Effective evaluation isn't easy; it involves all the lower levels of thinking skills. You have to remember, understand, and analyze information in order to make sound choices.

One way to help children develop the ability to evaluate effectively is to ask for their opinions about the things that affect them—political issues such as drug legalization and defense spending, local traffic regulations and age limits for driver's licenses, school discipline policies and dress codes, etc. If you haven't made a habit of talking to your child about what he or she thinks, you might not get a good response the first time. Don't give up. Tell your child that you are truly interested in what he or she thinks. Remind him or her that opinions are thoughts—they aren't carved in stone, and they can be changed. We learn by constantly reevaluating our opinions as we gain more information and experience. Give some examples of opinions you had or things you believed that you no longer believe and explain why you changed your mind about that subject or idea.

The subject matter of your discussions isn't as important as the thought process involved. Whether you're discussing where to go on your family vacation or whether capital punishment should be abolished, the key is to focus on thinking. Encourage your child to express her ideas and to explain why she believes certain things, what convinced her to arrive at a specific decision or point of view. It is difficult sometimes to keep from laughing or summarily dismissing young people's ideas as ridiculous—I will never understand, for example, why so many teens think a diamond stud imbedded in the side of somebody's nose is attractive—but children are sensitive (as I'm sure you know), and if they think you are laughing at them or not taking them seriously, they'll stop talking and you won't be able to help them develop good thinking skills because you won't know what they're thinking. Instead of criticizing or pointing out weaknesses in your child's logic, keep asking questions that require her to think more carefully, to analyze information, to compare different points of view. If you should happen to slip and laugh out loud, or hurt your child's feelings by dismissing his ideas as immature or silly, apologize immediately and use your own response as an example of how *not* to react to somebody else's ideas.

GIVE ME AN EXAMPLE

You can give your child a real boost toward good grades if you can teach him to give examples. Teachers are forever asking students to give specific examples to support their ideas and opinions, and students are forever responding with shrugs and blank looks. If you can help your child learn to support his or her statements with examples—from reading, conversations, experience, observation—you will be giving your child a big boost toward success in school. The higher the grade level, the more instructors will expect students to be able to support and defend their statements.

Here are some examples of how to ask children for examples. Let's say that you have a young child who claims not to like mustard, although that child has never tasted mustard. Many of us would respond with, "How do you know you don't like it if you haven't tried it?" The answer to that question would be, most likely, a shrug and refusal to discuss or taste mustard because we didn't really ask a question, we just made fun of the child. If you ask the child why he or she doesn't like mustard, you might be told, "Just because." I think "just because" is the answer children give when they don't know why they think something. If we point out that "just because" is a silly answer, we don't encourage thinking. If we say, "Let's see. What could there be about mustard that you don't like? The color? The smell? Does it remind you of some other food that you don't like?" then we prompt the child to think about why mustard isn't appealing. In the end, the child may still refuse to eat mustard, but we will have planted a seed of thought.

Here's another example. If a child says that the next-door neighbor is a nice man, or a mean man, the natural response would be to ask why. Again, you might get a shrug in response, or something like, "He always does this or always does that."

Nobody "always" does anything, so that is not a good example to support a statement. I would ask this child, "Did you see Mr. Neighbor do something to make you say that about him? Did somebody tell you about him? Do you think that person told the truth? Why would that person lie? Based on your own experience and observation, do you think Mr. Neighbor is nice or mean? Do you think there might be a reason for his behavior on a particular day?" By asking questions that require children to think about the sources of information, the validity of those sources, we can help them learn to be good critical thinkers.

READ ME A STORY

Reading is like any other skill—practice may not make perfect, but it certainly makes improvement. Ask your child to read to you whenever you have a few minutes. If you don't have time to sit down and watch your child read, ask her to read to you while you cook or wash dishes or check the stock market quotations on your computer. If you miss something and lose track of the story line, ask your child to repeat what you missed. Tell her that you are enjoying the story but were momentarily distracted. It happens to everybody. Thank your child for reading to you. It's a gift to give somebody a story.

Read to your children. (Even teenagers like to listen to a good story. So do most adults.) My junior and senior high school students used to beg me to read to them— everything from creepy-crawly Stephen King stories to fiction from *The New Yorker*. You don't have to be a professional speaker to capture your audience. A good story tells itself. You can help by using different voices for characters, slowing down during dramatic moments, creating excitement by raising and lowering your voice, or speaking very loudly or whispering where it fits the story. If you don't read very well, practice. You'll improve. I promise. If you simply can't bring yourself to read aloud, for whatever reason, ask a friend or relative, perhaps an older brother or a cousin, to read to your child.

WHAT IF *YOU* DON'T LIKE TO READ?

This is one case in which I would recommend being less than honest. For your child's sake, keep your dislike of reading to yourself. I will never forget the day that Durrell Love, an excellent student, refused to open his book and follow along as we read *The Taming of the Shrew*. The day before, Durrell had volunteered to read the role of Petruchio, and seemed to be enjoying himself. When I asked Durrell why he wasn't reading, he said, "Shakespeare is a waste of time. I told my mom about what we were reading last night and she said it's a waste of time. She read Shakespeare in school and never used it in her whole life." He refused to read or listen to the rest of the play, and his grade suffered. Your attitude toward school, and reading, has a very strong effect on your child's attitude, although you may never know it. Since reading is required for every academic subject, the more you encourage your child to read, the easier school will be. He or she may decide after graduation that reading is useless. Fine. But until then, reading is an important part of your child's school life, so it's in your child's best interest to read as well as possible.

By the way, I just have to add that I don't think any

knowledge is a waste of time. You may not apply every single thing you learn, but your brain is like a muscle—the more you use it, the stronger it gets. Every little bit of information your brain stores gives you that much more background, makes you that much more educated. Although I know many people who would be insulted to be called ignorant, I don't know a single person who would be insulted to be called educated.

Chapter 7

LEARNING STYLES

※

You've created the perfect study area for your child—a desk and chair in a quiet room with a bright light—but she never uses it. Instead, she does her homework lying on her stomach, peering over the edge of her bed at her schoolbooks that are stacked on the floor in the shadows. As she reads, she jiggles her feet to the beat of the song blaring from the radio. Can a child possibly concentrate under such conditions?

Your son insists that he studies better and earns higher grades if he reads his textbooks in the living room, with one eye on the television set and both ears tuned into his Walkman. Does he really expect you to believe him?

You tell your son to take out the trash, make his bed, and put his dirty socks in the hamper before he goes outside to play. He says, "Okay," and immediately takes out the trash, but ten minutes later you pass his bedroom and notice that his bed sheets are still on the floor next to a truckload of smelly socks—and he's outside tossing a Frisbee on the front lawn. When you remind him, he says he forgot, honest he did. Could an intelligent child truly forget a few simple tasks so quickly?

Yes. Yes. Yes. Recent studies prove that some people actually read more easily in dim light (without damaging their eyes) and concentrate better with background music to drown out distractions. Some students prefer to be surrounded by a variety of sights and sounds, which forces them to "tune out" everything except for the task at hand. Others seem to need to do two things at once. And even the most intelligent child will forget a list of spoken directions if that child depends on visual clues (such as a written list) as reminders.

BASIC LEARNING STYLES (PREFERENCES)

There are so many different theories and so many conflicting reports about how people learn that only one thing is certain—nobody knows for sure. What we do know, and the most recent studies confirm this again and again, is that different people learn in different ways. For example, some people learn best by listening and talking. Others like to see things for themselves. Still others need to do things in order to learn. We call these three basic learning styles *auditory* (hearing), *visual* (seeing), and *kinesthetic* (moving).

To illustrate these three basic learning styles or preferences, imagine that you need to travel from one point to another along a complicated route. You could receive directions in one of three ways. Which would you prefer?

1. Somebody gives you detailed verbal instructions directing you from point A to point B. As you are driving, you "hear" the instructions in your mind: Go south three miles, take a right, turn left at the second light.

2. You look at a map and memorize or familiarize yourself with the route you need to follow. You mark the route and "see" it in your mind as you are driving. You may be able to complete the trip without looking at the map, or you may glance at it for reference during your trip.

3. You make a test drive (in an actual car, or using a model car and a large map) from point A to point B with a passenger who gives you directions as you are driving. You may not know exactly where you are, but you know you could retrace the route after you have driven it once.

For most of us, one method will be much more appealing than the other two. I am a visual learner, so number 2 would be my first choice. I might be able to remember the route if I drove it once, but I would prefer to have a map and guide myself. Number 1 is not for me—I have a terrible time trying to follow verbal directions because I can never recall them exactly as they were spoken and I become very frustrated.

EVERY CHILD HAS A UNIQUE STYLE

Although most of us learn to use a combination of different styles, we tend to favor one particular style, even as infants. One toddler will ask for repeated instruction and help in tying his shoes while another insists on doing it himself, even if it takes an hour. One child will spend hours happily listening to an adult reading the same story over and over again, while her sister insists on holding the book, pointing at the words, and carefully inspecting each picture. Meanwhile, a third sister is dismantling the toys in the toy box, not because she is destructive, but because she needs to see how things work and she wants to work them herself. While these different play activities are going on, children are learning—at their own pace, in their own individual styles. Learning styles become much more important when children reach school age. Recent studies indicate that 40 percent of children learn by doing and only 12 percent of children learn by listening—but most school systems rely heavily on lectures and audio presentations.

When they start school, auditory learners adapt most easily to the classroom because listening and talking come naturally to them. Visual learners usually learn to adapt and frequently design their own methods for translating verbal instructions into pictures—by drawing, doodling, searching for illustrations in books, etc. Because colors and shapes play such a large role in the early years of school instruction, visual learners sometimes progress as far as junior high school before they encounter serious problems in school. Kinesthetic learners, the "doers," have the hardest time handling school lessons that are primarily based on following verbal instructions. For many years, people blamed students for being lazy or not trying hard enough, when sometimes that wasn't the case at all. Fortunately, there have always been teachers who instinctively recognize student needs and try to create lessons that meet the different needs of the students in a particular class. Eventually, the success of those teachers led others to study their methods. Today, more and more teachers, counselors, and administrators are becoming aware of the importance of recognizing and responding to differences in individual students' needs in the classroom.

WHAT'S YOUR CHILD'S STYLE?

How do you determine your child's learning style or preference? Sometimes simply understanding that learning preferences exist is enough for you to recognize them:

- Oh, yes. Now that you mention it, I realize that Susie always picks activities that involve movement—jigsaw puzzles, building blocks, jacks.
- Jerome watches the same videos over and over, and he loves to look at the family picture albums, pointing out the people he recognizes.
- Tamara memorizes the words to TV and radio commercials and likes to sing along. She often repeats fa-

vorite phrases that she has overheard and often surprises me by remembering casual remarks that I have made during the day.

It may seem that your child uses all three methods for learning, which is probably true, but if you observe closely, you will probably find that he or she prefers one style over the others. Be aware that if a child knows you are observing, he may choose specific behavior if that's what he thinks he is supposed to do or what he thinks you want him to do. If you say, "Would you like to read a story or watch a video?" your question may seem innocent. But if it is your practice to sit down and read with your child, but leave him alone to watch videos, he may choose the story just because he wants your company. You will probably get a truer picture of your child's learning style if you simply pay attention to the things he does throughout the day.

Here is one example: Think about the way your child responds to a new game. Does she listen carefully to instructions, and repeat them back to you, or ask you to repeat them to her? If so, she may be an auditory learner. Or does she prefer to watch other people play the game until she understands it and is ready to join? Most likely, she is a visual learner. Maybe she waves you away, insists she doesn't need instructions, and jumps right into the game, learning as she goes along—that's how kinesthetic learners approach new projects.

Note: you may read something to the effect that most kinesthetic learners are boys, or that girls tend to display better verbal skills at earlier ages than boys do, but I am not convinced that those generalizations are true. They could very well be learned behaviors. Certainly it is possible that some girls might prefer to learn by doing things and moving objects and some boys might prefer to learn by listening and talking. One of the worst things we can do is decide beforehand what is "normal." There is no such thing. When we label children, we stop seeing them as they actually are. A child who prefers to watch and learn before trying a new activity, for example, may be labeled as "shy" or "slow," when he or she simply needs time to process new information.

MORE CLUES TO A CHILD'S STYLE

Children give us so many clues about their learning preferences. Auditory learners (kids who learn by listening and talking) tend to remember people's names, but may forget their faces. They memorize the words to advertisements on the radio and TV and sing them repeatedly. They like to listen, but they like to talk, too, and they tend to give long, detailed explanations of their activities. They may take notes if you insist, but they'd rather study by repeating things out loud or listening to somebody else repeat them. Many children tune out the voice of the narrator when watching an instructional television program or videotape, but auditory learners listen to what's being said and remember much of the new information.

Kinesthetic learners, on the other hand, may not like to listen or talk. They don't remember the commercials because they are too busy doing something else while watching TV or listening to the radio. What they remember best are the things that they do. They may not remember what they read or are told about computers, even if you show them pictures, but they remember every single thing they do if they use a computer. Kinesthetic learners aren't fond of note taking, and usually won't use notes to study even if they are required to take them during class. This isn't because they're stubborn, but because written notes aren't very helpful to people who learn by movement and action.

Visual learners like to draw pictures and take notes. They remember what they see: signs, faces, words, demonstrations. They may like to talk, but they tend to become impatient if they are expected to listen for a long time, because they need to see the thing that's being discussed. Visual learners also tend to take more notes in school than other students do, and they use the notes to study. After watching a narrated videotape, visual learners may not remember any of the information they heard, but they will be able to describe what they saw in great detail.

If you'd like some expert help to determine your child's learning preferences and needs, your local school should be your first source. Some counselors and teachers have been trained to test and evaluate children's preferences. If you want an expert evaluation, you could contact the guidance or counseling office at your school and ask whether the staff is trained to evaluate learning styles or preferences. If your school counselors are not trained and cannot refer you to another agency, you might contact your school district office or the county office of education and ask for a referral. Another possible source of information is the education department of a local university. If you still can't find help, ask the reference librarian at your local public library to help you locate books or academic journals (when searching for information on a computer database, be sure to try different subject titles, such as learning styles, learning preferences, teaching styles, etc.). Some of the publications I have read and would suggest include: *Vocational Educational Journal, English Journal, Schools in the Middle, Educational Leadership, Principal*. I found the research and writings of Rita and Kenneth Dunn to be particularly interesting and helpful.

TEACH YOUR CHILD TO ASK FOR HELP

Okay, so you and your child have identified his learning style. Now what? How do you make use of this information?

The biggest benefit of knowing your child's learning style is that you both will understand that a child isn't "dumb" just because he has trouble learning some particular subject. When I was a junior in high school, I thought something had happened to my brain. Suddenly, I was stupid. In elementary and junior high school, I had loved math. Algebra I and II were a breeze, and Geometry was fun. But I failed every single lesson in Trigonometry and finally, tearfully, dropped out of the class. I didn't know what had happened, whether I had finally found my limit or somehow turned stupid during summer vacation. I felt so ashamed. It wasn't until years later, in college, when I discovered that I was a visual learner, that I understood what had happened to me. My other math teachers had used graphs and pictures to illustrate each new concept.

My trig teacher relied on lectures and verbal explanations. I couldn't "see" what he was teaching, and so I couldn't learn. Perhaps he could have taught me if I had known how to ask for his help.

That's where the second advantage of knowing your child's learning preference comes in: He or she can learn to ask for specific help from teachers. Since the automatic reaction of teachers, when questioned, is to repeat information in a louder voice, or more slowly, auditory learners usually don't need to do anything more than ask the instructor to repeat what she just said. But visual and kinesthetic learners need to learn how to ask for help. Here are some sample phrases that I teach to my students to help them prepare for talking to other teachers.

Visual learners may say:

- "I learn best when I can see some kind of picture of what I'm learning. Could you help me figure out how to present this concept in a drawing or graph or something I can see?"
- "I like to see things so I can learn better. Can you recommend a videotape about this particular topic? I'd like to watch it at home because I think it will help me."
- "I understand what you're saying, but I just can't 'see it' in my mind. Could you draw a picture on the board to illustrate this concept for me?"

Kinesthetic learners may say:

- "I learn the best when I can do things for myself. Could you help me go through a couple of these problems, step by step, while I do the work, so I can get the hang of it?"

- "I have a hard time learning things unless I can move around while I'm thinking. Would it be all right with you if I stand in the back of the class and walk around a little bit if I'm careful not to distract the other students?"

- "I'm one of those people who learn by moving and doing. I'm having a problem remembering this new information. Can you help me think of a way I can move things or do some activity to help me learn?"

A third advantage of knowing your child's learning style is that he or she can choose projects and subjects that make the best use of individual talents. When given a choice of projects for a grade in school, a kinesthetic learner can choose to give a demonstration instead of writing a paper. A visual learner can design collages, posters, or computer graphics—projects that will emphasize her skills and talents.

On the other hand, if a child believes that his preferred style puts him at a disadvantage—a kinesthetic learner who is struggling with history, for example—he can choose study activities that will help him improve his listening skills or design study aids, such as taping the teacher's classroom lectures, to help him prepare for exams.

LOOK AND LEARN

When your child is learning new material, you can concentrate on study methods that take advantage of a child's natural learning style. For visual learners, you'll want to emphasize images and color. Flash cards and posters are good study aids. You can make your own flash cards for vocabulary words, with the word on one side of the card and the definition on the other. Flash cards also work for learning lists of biological or mathematical terms. On the front of a card, print the question: *What is a right triangle?* or *What are the steps in photosynthesis?* Print the answers on the backs of the cards. You can print spelling lists in large letters and post them on a wall where your child will see them often. For a preschool child who tends toward the visual, you can use catalogs or magazines to build vocabulary and stimulate discussions by pointing to pictures and asking the child to name the object or describe the activity. You can also ask children to draw their own pictures to illustrate words, objects, and actions.

LISTEN AND LEARN

Although I am a visual learner, I sometimes rely on auditory skills to learn new information that involves a lot of unfamiliar terminology. In my high school biology class, I remember using music to learn the names of the bones in the human body. I made up songs to the tune of *Yankee Doodle* and memorized the songs. Then, during tests, I'd sing the songs to myself quietly and write down the information. Here's an excerpt from one of my Yankee Doodle biology songs:

My ulna and my radius hook up to my humerus
That makes up my arm, it's true, I'm absolutely serious.
My thighbones are my femurs, and my knees are my patellas
Tibia and fibula are my lower leg fellas.

In more modern times, I have met both students and teachers who use rap as a study technique. The repeating rhythms and meter of rap music can make it easier to remember large amounts of information. I know one very successful math teacher who raps out algebraic formulas, and her students learn them almost immediately.

This idea may sound silly to you, but it worked for me, and I have had many students use the same technique. It's the same principle as singing the ABC song most of us learned in kindergarten, the one that ends with "Now I know my ABCs, what do you think of me?" It's also the same reason that we sometimes get a song "stuck in our heads." I know you've heard an obnoxious jingle on the radio, one that you'd truly like to forget, and yet it keeps replaying in your mind throughout the day. Why not take advantage of our brain's ability to memorize words and music?

I'm not suggesting that making up songs will help anybody understand complicated concepts. Of course, that won't work. But making up songs can help us remember groups of unfamiliar terms. Once we jot down those terms, we have a key to jogging our memories for more information. Think of it as one of those word puzzles where you uncover one letter at a time. Each new letter gives another clue to the answer.

During homework and study time at home, auditory learners may benefit from reading their textbooks out loud or listening to audio tapes of the teacher's presentations. Instead of just looking at lists of spelling, vocabulary words, or history dates, auditory learners need to spell words out loud and repeat definitions or dates several times. Sometimes, a combination of writing words, definitions, or important dates down on paper while spelling or saying them will help reinforce learning.

MOVE AND LEARN

If your child is a kinesthetic learner, you'll want to try to incorporate movement—of your child or objects—into study time. If the lesson is basic addition and subtraction, you can use pennies or marbles or some other object that your child can manipulate. If the lesson is spelling, you might try "air writing," where your child uses his finger to write the words out. Sometimes movement itself is enough to stimulate the brain. I've had kinesthetic students who simply needed to stand up and move around (in the back of the room where they wouldn't distract others) while I was introducing a new idea to the class. I'd like to say that I was enlightened enough to suggest this option for those students, but unfortunately, it was a last resort. They simply couldn't sit still while I was introducing a new topic, no matter how hard they tried.

One boy I will never forget carried a pink rubber ball that had little tendrils, like a porcupine. Danny sat at his desk, tossing the ball from one hand to the other and rocking gently from side to side as I addressed the class. His ball tossing distracted me as well as the students seated near him. When I took the ball away and asked him to sit still, Danny nodded agreeably, but as soon as I resumed my instruction, he started percolating like a human coffeepot. His legs twitched and his fingers began drumming out a rhythm on his desktop. Again, I stopped, and asked Danny to stop drumming. He looked down at his fingers as though he'd never seen them before. He hadn't realized he'd been drumming. Eventually, exasperated, I tossed the ball back to Danny and told him to stand in the back of the room where he could toss to his heart's content without distracting the other students. It worked. Danny tossed his ball and shifted his weight from one foot to the other during my entire presentation—but he earned an A on the assignment for that lesson! After that, I gave students the option of standing silently in the back of the room, as long as they didn't disrupt anybody else's concentration.

DON'T IGNORE THE WEAKNESSES

Although I think it's helpful to focus on natural learning styles when new material is presented in school, I think it's a mistake to forget about the other styles of learning. The more versatile your child can become in using different learning styles, the better her chances of success in school. Some teachers still rely on a basic "chalk and talk" presentation that requires good listening skills, but more and more teachers are working to incorporate different teaching styles into their lessons. Still, no matter how hard we try, there are some concepts that we can't illustrate. After all these years, I still can't draw a picture of irony (at least not one that you'd recognize as such). So I would recommend helping your child improve her skills in her weakest areas.

LISTEN UP

If listening skills are your child's weak point, as they are for so many students, you can help her improve those skills by concentrating on exercises and games that require listening. A good way to improve listening skills and reading comprehension at the same time is to have your child listen to you read a story or newspaper article out loud, then answer questions about what you read.

You might want to try a game I've used in my classroom to help students improve listening skills. You can do this at home with a paper and pencil. Both you and your child need to sit at a desk or table, with your backs to each other so you can't see what is on the other person's paper. Your task is to draw a few circles, lines, boxes, and triangles on your paper so that you have a simple drawing. (Don't make your first drawing too complicated. You may be surprised how difficult this is to do with a very basic drawing.)

When your drawing is finished, your task is to give your child instructions so that he can draw a picture identical to yours. The trick is that neither of you is allowed to look at the other person's paper. You can't watch your child draw and correct him when he makes a mistake. He must rely entirely on your verbal instructions. When you have finished giving instructions, compare your two drawings. Next, trade places and have your child draw a picture and instruct you.

If you'd like a little help to get started, here is a sample drawing, with instructions:

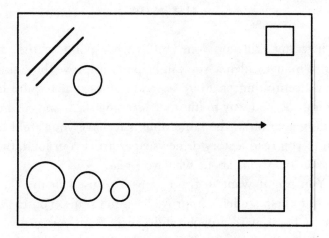

1. Place your paper on the desk so that it is longer than it is high
2. In the upper right corner of the page, draw a small square, about 1½ inches high.
3. In the upper left corner of the page, draw two parallel lines, about 2 inches long, that are situated diagonally to the corner, running from the left side to the top of the page.
4. About ½ inch below the two diagonal lines, draw a circle 1½ inches in diameter.

5. In the center of the page, draw a horizontal line from left to right, leaving a two-inch margin on each side of the page.
6. Draw an arrowhead on the right end of the center line, pointing to the right.
7. In the lower left corner of the page, starting at the left, draw three circles, making each circle slightly smaller than the one before. The circle on the left should be the biggest, and it should measure about 2 inches in diameter. The next circle should be 1½ inches, the third circle 1 inch.
8. In the lower right corner of the page, draw a square that is about twice as big as the square in the upper right corner.

If your drawing looks anything like the sample, you've done very well.

You can also practice listening skills by giving your child a list of physical movements to perform. For example, you could read this list of instructions:

Walk ten paces forward and stop.
Look to your left, then your right.
Stomp your left foot twice.
Clap your hands once.
Place your right hand over your right ear and count to thirty by twos.

If your child makes a mistake, repeat the instructions and let her try again. If this seems too easy, you can add more movements to the list, or make the instructions more complicated.

Now, here's an example of a more complicated task. You can give these instructions one at a time, or for a real challenge, read all the instructions and see whether your child can remember them in sequence.

Instructions:

1. Print your name, last name first, in the upper right corner of a sheet of paper.
2. Rotate the paper one-quarter turn so that your name is in the lower right corner.
3. Turn the paper over without rotating it.
4. Write the number "99" in the upper right-hand corner.
5. Turn the paper back over so that your name is in the upper right again.
6. Fold up the lower left corner. Your number should appear right side up.

Your page should look something like this:

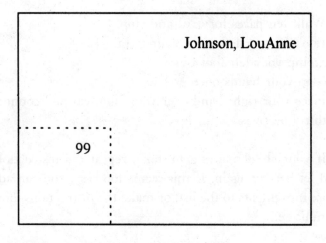

THERE'S MORE TO SEE

To develop better visual skills, you can create similar games. Here's one of my childhood favorites. While your child is out of the room, place fifteen to twenty small objects (a spool of thread, a spoon, two pennies, an egg, a pencil, and so on) on the top of a table. Bring your child into the room and let him look at the objects for thirty seconds. Then have him go into another room and write down the names of as many objects as he can remember. Depending upon the age and ability of your child, you may want to add or subtract a few objects, or give your child more or less time to look at the objects.

Another way to practice visual skills is to walk into an unfamiliar room and look around for a minute. Then leave and try to describe the room: the color of the walls and whether they are painted or papered; the color and texture of the floor and ceiling; the number and design of light fixtures; the size, color, and design of any furniture in the room; any artwork or notices posted on the walls; a complete description of any people, including height, weight, hair color, eye color, clothing, glasses, fingernails, jewelry, and so forth. After you've written down everything you remember, go back into the room to check the accuracy of your notes and see how many things you didn't notice.

The best thing about using these games to practice listening, moving, and seeing is that they give you a chance to spend time with your child in a fun activity. Two more pluses—they don't cost anything but your time and they are limited only by your imagination. That's a true bargain in my book.

WORKING WITH THE TEACHER

Most teachers make a sincere effort to incorporate different teaching styles into their lesson plans, so they can reach all their students. But it isn't always easy, and sometimes it's downright impossible, to figure out how to teach a particular concept in a visual or kinesthetic style. Be tactful if you decide to approach your child's teacher about his or her teaching methods. Don't begin by criticizing the teacher or making suggestions. (Imagine how you would feel if the teacher came to your workplace and told you how to do your job.) Instead, explain that you are trying to understand how your child learns, and that you want to work with the teacher to help your child learn better.

If your attempts to communicate with your child's teacher fail, but your child is still passing that teacher's class, I wouldn't worry too much. No, your child may not earn the grade he or she could have earned with a different teacher, but learning to get along with difficult people is an important lesson. Perhaps your child will have to work harder than he would with a different teacher, but hard work won't hurt him. He can still learn the subject matter well by using textbooks and good study habits. And I honestly believe that as long as a child understands that it isn't entirely his or her fault that a particular subject or class is difficult—that it may be due to a discrepancy between the child's learning style and the teacher's teaching style—then no permanent damage will result. When a child believes it's his fault, that he's bad or dumb or unteachable, we have true cause for worry.

Chapter 8

A LITTLE PSYCHOLOGY GOES A LONG WAY

YOU'RE THE EXPERT

There is a little bit of psychologist in all of us. *Not me*, you say? I would disagree, even though I haven't met you. If you are a parent, guardian, or adult relative of a child, I would bet you have done at least one (and maybe even two!) of the following:

- Challenged a picky eater with a variation of "Bet you can't eat all those carrots"
- Pretended to yawn and fall asleep on the bed beside a reluctant napper to get him to join the slumber party
- Promised $5 or $10 or $20 for every A on a child's report card
- Threatened to ground a child unless his grades improved on the next report card

- Offered to read a story in order to lure a little nightowl into bed
- Bit your tongue to keep from criticizing your child's hair/clothes/music/friends
- Told a child, "I'm so ashamed of you!" or "I'm so proud of you!"

Every one of those things involves the use of psychology. Bribery, threats, rewards, praise, criticism, challenges, setting examples—all are different forms of psychological manipulation. I'm not using the word *manipulation* in its negative sense, but rather in the sense that we adults use mental strategies to convince children to do what we want them to. Sometimes our psychology works, and sometimes it backfires. I believe we have a much greater chance of success if we first figure out *why* a child behaves a certain way before we try to change the behavior. Unless we understand what motivates a child's behavior, it's very difficult to come up with a more persuasive alternative. I've probably said this before, since I say it often, but it bears repeating: *There is a reason for everything a child does.* The reason may not make sense to you or me, and sometimes it doesn't make sense to the child, but there is a reason, nevertheless.

WHY DO SMART KIDS FAIL?

Here's an example of a common problem. Let's imagine that you have an intelligent, able child who is earning poor grades. What should you do? You have so many options that I can't list them all, but here are a few. You could threaten to ground the child or take away privileges if the grades don't improve, you could have a heart-to-heart talk, you could offer money or a special treat for a better grade, you could call the teacher and request a conference, and so on. You might be lucky. Your plan might work, but you'd have to wait until the next reporting period to find out. If you chose the wrong option, you would have lost valuable time and would have to start back at square one.

What would I do in this situation? I have tried many different things, but I've never done the same thing twice, because there was a different reason every time one of my students failed my class or someone else's. Here are just a few of those reasons:

- Zack refused to turn in his history assignments because his girlfriend was assigned to a different class period for the same subject, and Zack wanted to switch class periods so they could be together. The guidance office wouldn't approve the change, so Zack tried to fail history in the hope that the teacher would kick him out of class and the guidance office would be forced to place him in the other section.

- Marisol had been accosted three times in the girls' rest room by two older girls who were repeating the same class as Marisol. The older girls were upset because Marisol had high grades and had been offered a scholarship upon graduation, while they were not going to graduate at all because they had failed so many classes. They threatened to hurt Marisol if she didn't stop earning high grades, and they said they would beat up her younger sister if she told any adults about their threats.

- Reza earned very high grades when he remembered to do his assignments, but his grades suffered because of his lack of organization. Even when he made notes to remind himself, he often lost the notes and forgot about the assignments. At the beginning of the grading period, Reza would turn over a new leaf, but before long he'd begin floundering and failing. He'd become discouraged, then despondent, then apathetic.

- Tyeisha intentionally failed tests and disrupted classes because whenever her mother became overwhelmed, she would called Tyeisha's father (the couple were divorced) to come to town and help her "handle" Tyeisha. After several months, Tyeisha finally confided to me that she hoped her parents would reunite if she kept bringing them together. Both parents were happily remarried, but Tyeisha refused to give up hope.

- Brian stopped working halfway through his senior year and sat like a lump in class. His parents, counselors, and I tried talking to him, but all we got were shrugs in return. Finally, when it was too late to make up the missed work and failed exams, Brian admitted that he was afraid to graduate. He didn't know what to do with his life. He didn't think he was smart enough to go to college and he hadn't been able to find a job. He hoped he could stay in school for another year while he decided what to do.

- Araceli's grades dropped in every class when her father suddenly decided that she could no longer do homework or read books at home because he didn't want her to go to college. He was upset because his wife had started going to night school to earn her GED and he was threatened by the idea of the women in his family becoming educated and independent. He feared they would lose respect for him.

NOBODY WANTS TO FAIL

During my first year as a teacher, some of the older teachers told me not to waste so much of my time and energy on students who chose to fail. Some kids are just lazy, they said, and you can't force a child to succeed. Perhaps some of those students were lazy, but it has never made sense to me that a child would choose to fail. Nobody wants to be a failure. So I believe that if they fail, there is a reason, and if I find the reason, I might be able to offer some solution. I'm not always successful, but I am successful often enough to convince me that it's worth the effort to keep trying.

In case you are interested in how I handled the cases I mentioned, here is a brief synopsis of my "solutions."

I called Zack and his girlfriend, Gloria, into my office to talk. Gloria did not know that Zack had been purposely failing history. She had believed his excuse that it was the teacher's fault, and she believed that Zack's grades would improve if he were in the same class with her. When Gloria discovered what Zack had been doing, she told him to "grow up." I thought Zack might have been too proud to continue the discussion after Gloria's comment, but he blushed gracefully and apologized to me. I suggested that he apologize to his history teacher. That was too much for Zack, but he did bring up his grade enough to pass the course.

I learned about Marisol's predicament when she came to class with bleeding scratch marks on her neck. When I insisted on escorting her directly to the nurse's office, Marisol burst into tears and told me the whole story. We met with the principal and one of the counselors and discussed alternative solutions. Marisol filed a restraining order against one of the girls, who was eighteen years old. She started keeping a journal to record any further verbal or physical assaults, with signatures of any witnesses to the assaults. Two other senior girls volunteered to escort Marisol to and from her classes until the end of the year. The girls who had been tormenting Marisol sometimes followed her at a distance, and occasionally made insulting remarks in the hallways, but did not cause any more serious trouble. Marisol graduated and went to college on a scholarship.

Reza's problem didn't require a lot of time or energy. I took him to a stationery store and helped him choose a daily planning calendar. He carried the calendar to all of his classes (yes, some of the other students teased him and called him Mr. Executive, but he handled it). At the end of each class period, Reza wrote down the homework assignment and any upcoming projects or exams on his calendar. At first, he left his calendar behind on his desk in somebody's classroom at least twice a week, but he eventually got used to carrying it with him and his grades and attitude improved.

Tyeisha didn't tell me what was going on. By accident, I overheard her telling a friend about her plan. When I told Tyeisha that I knew what she was doing, and that I didn't think it would work, she started crying and collapsed into her seat. I suggested that she talk to the school psychologist and ask for some suggestions to help her accept her parents' situation. I also encouraged her to write about her feelings in her private journal. Although she tore up the pages after she wrote, Tyeisha said the writing helped, although she still prayed at night that her parents would divorce and remarry each other.

Brian's story doesn't have such a happy ending. He refused all offers of help and fell so far behind that he wasn't able to bring up his grades and graduate on time. The following year, he grew depressed over having to complete the same classes again, and dropped out of school. His mother told me he had a part-time job, but refused to go to counseling or GED classes.

Araceli's story, on the other hand, has a storybook ending. When we learned about her father's no-study rule, some other teachers and I arranged for two more classes to be added to Araceli's schedule. I'll admit it; we lied to her parents. We told them that she had to take the classes to make up for her low grades. We made one class period a study hall during which Araceli completed the homework she couldn't do at home. The only class available seventh period was art. Araceli turned out to be such a talented painter that she earned a scholarship to San Jose State University! The last time I spoke with her, she had completed her third year of college, but had changed her major to bilingual education—she's going to be a teacher.

I'm not saying it's easy. It takes a lot of time and energy—more than some parents have to give. Even if you have the time, it isn't easy to persuade students to articulate their reasons for failure. Sometimes they seem as surprised as I am when we sit down to talk and they finally figure out what they're doing. Other times, they know exactly what they're doing, but they are ashamed and don't want to admit it. That's why it's so important to try not to judge them. I keep reminding myself, "They act like children because they *are* children."

YOU'RE NEVER TOO OLD FOR JELL-O

You would think that high school seniors would be too sophisticated to fall for the "bet you can't eat all those carrots" approach, wouldn't you? I thought so, but decided to give it a try. This class complained repeatedly about having to write sentences for their vocabulary words, about having to complete so many review worksheets before each test. They didn't need to do "all that dumb stuff," they insisted. One day, as I distributed the review worksheet and the moans and groans became deafening, I made them all put down their pens and pencils and fold their hands on their desktops.

"I'm listening to you," I said. "You're absolutely right. You are very smart. You can learn these words without all that work. You don't need to do all this matching and fill in the blanks with the right word and write sentences using the new words. So, we're not going to do this review worksheet. We're just going to look it over. You'll pass the test tomorrow anyway." In the back of the room, I saw a boy pick up his pencil.

"No writing!" I said loudly. "I'm serious. You aren't allowed to write on this worksheet, and please don't argue with me."

"Aw, come on, Miss J," one of the boys said, "we know

what you're doing. You're trying to use child psychology on us."

"I wouldn't dream of trying that on you," I said. "You guys are too sharp to fall for that stuff, but I already made this worksheet and I didn't want all that time and effort to go to waste, so I thought I'd just let you look it over."

"Can't we just do the matching?" one girl asked. "I think I can get them all right."

"Nope," I said. "You can't write on these worksheets. Quit begging. You are not allowed to do this work. You're too smart to waste your time this way."

Of course, they ended up doing the worksheet. They knew they had been fooled, but they couldn't resist.

THE ODDS ARE WITH YOU

"Kim is too smart," one mother told me. "She figures out a way around everything I say or do." Maybe you believe your child is smarter than you are (maybe she is), but you are older and have the benefit of years of experience. Take advantage of your own experience to predict your child's behavior. How did you respond when your parents punished you? Did you repent and reform? If so, what was it that made you responsive to their punishment? If you didn't repent, but became angry and determined to exact revenge, what did they do wrong? What would have made you cooperate more readily? How did you feel when they criticized your posture, your speech, your attitude? If you honestly can't recall any of your childhood feelings, then try to put yourself in your child's place and look at the situation from a different perspective. Imagine that your boss at work treated you the way you are treating your child. How would you respond? It's not that much different. At work, the employer has the control, sets the rules, and can directly affect the workers' attitudes and happiness. At home, parents have much of the same power.

When you have an intelligent child who is determined to self-destruct, it is tempting to give up. The thing that keeps me going is that I know, in my heart, my desire to see them succeed is stronger than their desire to fail. On the occasion that you encounter a child who wants to fail more than you want him to succeed, he is going to fail. If a child decides to devote his boundless energy and hours of free time trying to fail or upset you, the child will win the battle. At that point, you can call in the experts for help, remind your child that you love him, cross your fingers, and hope your child will be satisfied with being a failure for only a short period of time.

YOUR TEACHER WHO LOVES YOU

One day, as I distributed a vocabulary exam to my students, I announced, "This exam was brought to you by your teacher who loves you and wants you to be successful in life." Instead of the usual chorus of complaints that precede any exam, my students giggled and rolled their eyes at each other. They were still smiling at the end of the class period, and several of them waved good-bye and called, "Good-bye, teacher who loves us. See you tomorrow." Having spent quite a bit of time around teenagers, I knew those good-byes were a hint. I realized that my students liked being reassured that I cared about them. From that day, I have referred to myself as Your Teacher Who Loves You in all of my classes.

Your children may know you love them, but they need to hear it. I can't tell you how many students have complained that their parents don't really love them, not because of any particular action or neglect, just because they feel unloved. I remember asking my own mother, repeatedly, whether my father loved me. "Of course, your father loves you very much," she always answered. Now that I'm older, I realize that my father did, indeed, love me very much, but he never told me. He had been raised to believe that fathers were supposed to be good providers and strict disciplinarians, and that displays of emotion were for softies.

I think it would be a wonderful idea if parents referred to themselves as Your Mother (Father) Who Loves You. Why not try it? I think you'll be pleasantly surprised at the response you'll receive from your child if, instead of saying, "No, you can't go to the party and that's final," you say, "I'm sorry you can't go to the party, but your father who loves you doesn't want you to go to unchaperoned parties because he wants you to be safe and healthy and grow up to be a happy adult, at which time you can go to all the parties you want."

And imagine the reaction you'd get if you didn't say, "No, you can't go hang around with your friends because I need to know where you are," and said this instead: "Your mother who loves you wants to know exactly where you are going and who will be with you, not because she doesn't trust you, but because the world can be dangerous and she doesn't always trust other people not to hurt her precious, lovable child."

LAUGHTER IS THE BEST DEFENSE

You've probably figured out already that my sense of humor is my biggest weapon in the war against ignorance, illiteracy, and bad attitudes among schoolchildren. It didn't take long for me to learn that I couldn't bully my students into cooperating with me. Okay, sometimes I could bully them—but it wasn't worth the effort because they always came back looking for revenge and the whole cycle started again. One sunny afternoon, as I passed out an assignment to my juniors, one of the biggest boys in class decided he wasn't going to participate. Instead, he thought he'd play Irritate the Teacher.

"I don't feel like doing this assignment," he challenged me. "What are you going to do about it?" I didn't hesitate. Immediately, I walked to his side and fell to my knees. Placing my palms together in an attitude of prayer, I said, "Oh, please do the assignment. I'm an old woman. Don't make me beg. It's so unattractive."

Completely embarrassed, the boy waved me away. "Get out of here," he mumbled, his cheeks bright red. Everybody in class was looking at him.

"If I get out of here, will you do the assignment? Please?" I asked. "It takes so little to make an old woman happy."

"All right," he said. "I'll do it. Just go."

He had wanted attention, but not that much. He did the assignment along with the rest of the students. After that encounter, I was dangerous. If I sent them to the office, they might not go. Or they might come back angry and waiting for a chance to get even. If I threatened them with bad grades, they might give in, grudgingly, or they might take the low grade, but I knew they'd pay me back sooner or later. But if I made them laugh, and told them I loved them, they couldn't win.

A few weeks after my discovery of humor as the ultimate weapon, two wannabe gangsters walked into my classroom wearing baggy pants, white sleeveless undershirts, and dark sunglasses. They took their seats in the back of the class, folded their arms across their chests, and struck a practiced pose. Their silent challenge was clear: "Try to make me take off my shades, Teacher. Just try." These were not friendly boys; they had managed to keep me at a distance, arriving at the last minute before the tardy bell rang, and leaving as soon as the dismissal bell sounded. I didn't know them very well, but I knew they were trying to let me know who was boss.

I remember thinking, "Go ahead and wear your sunglasses, you little stinkers, we're going to watch a movie today and you won't be able to see a thing." I didn't need to make an issue of the sunglasses, but I knew I needed to respond to the challenge or they would up the ante to try to force me into a confrontation. Suddenly, inspiration struck. As I introduced the video to the class and discussed the ideas I wanted them to think about while watching it, I strolled casually to the back of the room until I was standing directly behind the two boys. When I finished the introduction, I paused for a minute, then started singing very softly, "*Nunca hablo a ti con la mentira. Siempre hablo a ti con la verdad. Quisiera que olvides el pasado, que vuelvas a mi lado, que tengas compasión.*" [*Translation:* I will never lie to you. I will always tell you the truth. I want you to forget the past, return to my side, to have some compassion.] As I sang, my voice grew louder, and I finished the stanza with my hands clasped to my chest. Then I winked at my two gangsters, gave them a thumbs up, and quickly walked to the front of the room and started the video.

They tried, but they couldn't hold back their laughter. They shook their heads and exchanged glances that said, "She's loco, but what are we going to do?" By the time the first five minutes of the video had elapsed, they had both removed their sunglasses and were engrossed in the movie. How can you hate a woman who sings to you in your native tongue?

I highly recommend the use of humor to defuse arguments and prevent confrontations. I'm not saying you should never argue, but sometimes children will provoke arguments to create a smoke screen. If Bobby can get you to focus on his bad language, for example, you might forget to ask about his homework. Or if Sherry can entice you into yelling at her, she can run to her room, slam the door, and hope you'll give her time to cool off—and time to brush her teeth and wash her hair so you won't smell the smoke from the cigarette she shared with a friend after school.

IS IT REALLY PEER PRESSURE?

It's time to get serious for a minute. I think peer pressure takes far too much credit in this country for our children's behavior. I don't think it's that simple. Friends do have a tremendous effect on people's behavior, nobody can argue with that. In fact, I think sometimes adults are even more susceptible to peer pressure than children are. Peer pressure doesn't magically disappear when you turn twenty-one or thirty-five or when you have children. But, regardless of age, there are some people who manage to resist whatever temptations other people offer, and I think that's the important point. Why do some children manage to resist the temptation to lie or cheat, drink or take drugs, join gangs or have sex? What makes some young people so much stronger than others? Of course, people have different personalities, different desires and needs, but all of us have some basic needs. Psychologist Abraham Maslow developed a theory that is generally accepted as an accurate articulation of our basic human needs.

According to Maslow's Hierarchy of Needs, humans must satisfy their lower level needs before moving to higher level needs. As each level of need is fulfilled, time and energy are freed to focus on the next level. (Don't let the term *hierarchy* throw you—it simply means listing things in some kind of order, in this case from lowest to highest.)

Maslow's Hierarchy of Needs

1. **Physical needs (food, water, shelter, and so on):** If you were starving, or freezing, or dying of thirst, all

of your energy would be focused on trying to find food, shelter, or water.

2. **Safety (avoiding injury or harm):** Once your physical needs are met, you can afford to think about things like avoiding harm. If you were starving, for example, you would probably risk danger to find food. With a full stomach, you might think twice about taking chances with your life.

3. **Social (the feeling of being loved and accepted, of belonging to a group):** People (and a lot of animals) need to belong to a group and to feel loved. You can have a family and still feel unloved, however. That's why children spend time with people they don't really like or do things they know are wrong—they want to be accepted.

4. **Ego (having self-respect, feeling important):** Once we feel secure about being loved and having a place where we belong, we start to look for ways to increase our self-esteem and self-respect. We want to be winners, to earn attention, and to enjoy successes.

5. **Self-actualization (working to improve oneself, to learn for the sake of learning):** You have food, shelter, people who love you, self-respect—now you're cooking! You're ready to develop your talents, learn things just for fun, exercise your brain, spend time helping other people, and so on.

Maslow's Hierarchy in Action   Until their lower level needs are met, children cannot move up to the next step in emotional and psychological development. A child who is hungry, for example, can't sit down and concentrate on learning how to read. He needs something to eat first, so he can focus his energy on words. Children who are afraid for their safety, who suffer from physical or emotional abuse, who are insecure about the stability of their parents' relationships, have a difficult time concentrating on schoolwork. I'm not suggesting that if you are in the midst of a separation or divorce you are hurting your child, but I am saying that they need to be reassured that they will be safe and protected no matter what happens. Children tend to think that the world revolves around them, and therefore, everything that happens is their fault.

How can you help your child move to the third level of needs? Provide safety, security, and love. Tell him repeatedly that you love him. Don't assume that your child knows you love her because you provide food, clothing, and shelter. Tell her that she is important, that you are keeping an eye out for her, that you are doing your best to keep her safe from harm. Tell him that you need him as part of your family, that you need him to trust you, to talk to you, to tell you when circumstances or people scare him. Hug him. Hug her. Every day. If you haven't made a habit of hugging your child, start now.

Human touch is very important to children's healthy development. Numerous psychological studies, ranging from the 1950s through the present, indicate that not only do children suffer from impaired cognitive (thinking) and motor (physical) skills if they don't receive affectionate touch, but babies will often die if they are deprived of affection. In one five-year study of orphaned babies who received adequate food, clothing, and shelter but no affection from their caretakers, one-third of the children died during the first year of the study. Their deaths were attributed to the lack of affection and human touch.

Don't despair if you haven't been hugging your child regularly. According to the *Concise Encyclopedia of Psychology* (1987, John Wiley & Sons, New York), there is strong evidence that slow mental and physical development caused by infant experiences can be repaired later on by "sustained effort or change in life experiences." Because we believe in the power of touch, when my stepchildren stay with us, my husband and I both give them "smart hugs" several times each day. Of course, we have no scientific proof that our hugs have made them smarter, but they are noticeably calmer and happier since we began our amateur therapy.

Children aren't the only people who benefit from hugs. While at the local university library recently, I ran across several journal articles that described hug therapy programs at nursing homes. One nursing staff even instituted a "hugging week" because their patients had such a positive response. Residents, family, and staff members all reported positive effects from the hug therapy. So, if you're uncomfortable or embarrassed by displays of affection, you can always rationalize your behavior as scientific research. Whatever you call it, hug those children, please.

If you'd like to read more about this topic, I'd suggest starting with the *Encyclopedia of Psychology* published by John Wiley & Sons as a reference source. If your library has a CD-ROM on-line computer system, check the PsychLit section for entries under "infant deprivation" and "infant development."

HUG ME

Sometimes I have been criticized for hugging students, but I stand behind my actions. I don't grab children or fondle them or hug them inappropriately. In fact, I think children can only learn to distinguish between appropriate and inappropriate touching if they are touched appropriately. I tell my students, "Nobody has the right to touch you if you don't want to be touched, including adults. If someone does touch you and you don't like it, tell the person. If he or she doesn't listen, tell somebody else." But when a child is upset or angry or feeling left out or unloved, an arm around his shoulder or a pat on her back, sometimes a gentle hug, can help him or her cope with overwhelming emotions. I have had several students who fidgeted nonstop during class and had trouble settling down to work unless I made some sort of contact with them before class began. When I touched those students, they would immediately calm down, although I'm sure they were unaware of what was taking place. Sometimes all I had to do was place my hand on the student's shoulder for a second and say, "Hello." Sometimes I'd shake hands and joke, "Welcome to English class. It's a pleasure to have you here today." Other times, I would simply place my hand over a child's hand and make eye contact, just to let her know I was happy to see her. I think you would be amazed at the difference even a brief touch can make in a child's attitude.

TOUCH ME NOT

Everybody has times when they don't want to be touched. At those times, a pat or a hug is irritating, not soothing. Sometimes we need our distance as much as we need love, and some people, including children, don't like to be touched very often at all. The reason is not as important as their right to be treated with respect. If a student makes it clear that he doesn't want anybody to touch him, I don't argue and I support his right to maintain his distance from other students. But sometimes children don't really mean it when they protest. Boys are particularly prone to pretending they are too cool or too tough to need or enjoy a hug. When my husband and I were newlyweds, my stepson Sean, who is twelve, used to protest loudly and wriggle away whenever I tried to hug him good-night. I didn't realize at the time that Sean always stood nearby, watching and giggling, while I hugged the other kids. Finally, one night, I gave up. I didn't even try to hug Sean. I hugged everybody else and shooed them all off to bed. Sean made several excuses to come out of his room that night. First, he had to get a glass of water. Then he needed to know what time we planned to get up in the morning. Next he wanted to know what we were having for breakfast.

After Sean's third appearance, I asked my husband, "What in the world is wrong with Sean tonight?" Mike winked at me and said, "I think he wants a hug." I didn't think Mike was right, but a few minutes later, when Sean reappeared, I said, "Sure, honey, I'll give you a hug." Sean said, "No," but didn't make even the tiniest effort to move away while I hugged him. He said, "Good-night, you guys" and went off to bed. It's been three months since then, and Sean doesn't even bother to pretend anymore. Sometimes he even gets in line twice for a bedtime hug!

If you try to hug your child and he or she protests, pay attention. Is he serious? Or is he complaining loudly while smiling sheepishly? Does her facial expression match her words? Or is she simply embarrassed by her (or your) emotions? You know your child. You can tell whether or not your hug is truly unwelcome. If it is, then I wouldn't press the issue. If you haven't had a close relationship with your child, it may take you time to develop the mutual trust you'll need to make you both comfortable with touching and hugging. But, trust me, deep inside your child wants to be hugged. All children need love and acceptance, but sometimes they are afraid they aren't going to get it. In that case, they try to pretend they don't care. The more afraid they are, the harder they pretend. It is my theory that the tougher a child tries to act, the softer the heart that child is trying to protect.

LOVE AND ACCEPTANCE

Many children become stuck at level three—the need to feel loved and accepted. These children may have families who love them very much, yet they don't feel loved. I can't tell you how many times a student has written in his private journal, "My parents don't care about me" when I know for a fact that the student's parents love him very much indeed. Sometimes, no matter what you do, your child won't feel loved and accepted, won't feel a true sense of belonging to your family. Other times, a child will reject his or her family. How to handle this situation if it occurs in your family will be up to you—whether to try to work it out yourselves, seek counseling, or wait patiently for the child to grow up. Perhaps it will help to know you aren't the Lone Ranger.

If you have a child who feels unloved or refuses to participate in the family, tell him you love him anyway. Tell her that you don't like her behavior, but that you still love her. Then, encourage this child to join some sort of group—a sports team, school club, neighborhood club, church choir, school chorus or band, scouts, a garage band, a 4-H program. It doesn't have to be an organized group. Two children who walk to school together or who sing in the school chorus together can create a minigroup that may satisfy their need to be accepted by their peers. Children who don't have a strong sense of family, and who don't belong to some kind of group, are the prime target for gangs, unhealthy love affairs, and dangerous friendships. They don't become involved in dangerous, unhealthy, or illegal activities because they are bad children, but because they think those things will fulfill a basic human need.

It may sound simplistic, but I think it's worth a try to simply ask your child, "Do you feel like an important member of our family?" or "Do you feel loved and accepted by our family?" If your child says, "No," it doesn't mean you are a bad parent or that your child has a problem—it simply means that your family is like a lot of other families. For some children, growing up is a difficult, painful process, and nobody seems to understand.

If your child won't talk to you, and you aren't sure

about what groups or clubs he or she may belong to in school, you can call the guidance office and ask to speak to a counselor. Explain that you don't want your child to think you are spying, but that you would like your conversation to remain confidential, between you and the counselor. Ask if she can check your child's record and see whether he or she belongs to any groups. Depending on the size of the school and the number of counselors, the counselor may know your child personally and may be able to tell you who your child associates with during school hours. If the counselor can't help, try a teacher. Ask who your child sits with in class, and whether he or she has any special friend or group of friends. Find out as much as you can about the friend(s). There is an old adage that goes something like, "Show me who your friends are and I will tell you who you are." In high school, that is particularly true, because teens tend to separate themselves into distinctly defined groups that usually share a common attitude toward school, parents, drugs, sex, and so on. Your child's friends don't have to be the best students in class, or the snappiest dressers, to be good kids, but teachers can usually tell you which groups tend to cut classes, smoke behind the school, attend wild parties, kiss in the hallways, etc.

If you find out that your child seems happy in school, with a best friend or a group of friends who cooperate most of the time and earn decent grades, I wouldn't worry too much (although I would try very hard to make a connection at home and improve communications there). On the other hand, if you learn that your child spends all his time alone, or frequently associates with students who earn bad grades or cut classes frequently or who cause disruptions and get into fights, then I think your child is asking for attention. I know this can be particularly frustrating when you are offering attention that your child refuses to accept.

I wish I could offer a solution, but there isn't any one solution that will work for every family. I would start with the teacher. She may be willing to try to talk with your child—sometimes students get themselves into situations they can't get out of themselves and they will gratefully accept help when it's offered. You may ask the guidance counselor if it would be possible to change your child's class schedule so that he will be with different students. You may want to request a conference with the counselors, one or more teachers, your child, and you. Your child may reject you even more strongly, but I think it would be worse to do nothing. Whatever you choose, I would suggest telling your child that you are worried about him and that you'd like to help him, but you don't know how. Sometimes a little honesty is enough to disarm a child. Your honesty may be met with no response. It doesn't mean your child isn't listening. Most likely, it means the opposite. But children are often taken by surprise when an adult is completely honest, and they don't know what to say.

I think one of the worst things you can do is to forbid your child to be friends with anybody. Children want very badly to be grown up, to be able to make decisions for themselves. When we intervene, they aren't thankful, and they don't "see the light." They become insulted and indignant that we would have the nerve to question their intelligence and judgment. My mother was clever. If I had a friend she didn't like, she never told me. Instead, she would involve me in conversations about her own school days, and talk about the friends she'd had. She'd manage to bring my own friends into the conversation without my noticing it, and she'd ask me questions that made me look at my friends differently. Eventually, after I found a new friend, my mother would tell me how smart I was, what good judgment I had. Once I said, "But if you didn't like Janie, why didn't you tell me?" My mother smiled and said, "If I had told you I didn't like her, you would have liked her even more just to prove me wrong. I'm right, aren't I?" She was right.

PEER PRESSURE CAN BE POSITIVE

Peer pressure doesn't have to be negative. I have seen students use positive peer pressure to create changes in their school and in their own lives. After some racial disturbances at one high school, a small group of students from different ethnic backgrounds joined together and established a kids-only club, no adults allowed. They met during lunch hour and talked about ways they could help other students learn to get along with different people. Although I wasn't permitted to attend any meetings, I saw more and more students join the group, which they dubbed Students United.

Another group of students started their own smoke-free, drug-free, alcohol-free party circuit, with their parents' support. Each weekend, they planned a party for the group at a student's home. Students brought chips and snacks, and the parents of the host provided drinks.

At the same high school, parents were involved in helping students arrange for an all-night After-Prom party and a Morp. The After-Prom party was created to give students a safe place to go where they could show off their fancy clothes, dance, play games, eat, and drive home sober. The Morp (Prom spelled backward) was for the kids who couldn't afford or didn't want to go to the prom. The Morp charged no admission (local businesses and parents paid for it). It provided a carnival-style party with a lot of games and food, and the kids wore their favorite grungy clothes. Both parties were drug-, alcohol-, and smoke-free and both had a very high attendance. Those parents proved that if you give kids the chance to choose a safe environment, most of them will.

CHECK YOUR EXPECTATIONS

I'm sure you've heard the stories about teachers who were told that their students were gifted when they were actually "average" students, and because the teachers' expectations were so high, the students performed at the "gifted" level. And you've probably heard stories of champion athletes who routinely meditate, closing their eyes and "seeing" themselves perform difficult feats. No doubt, you've seen the best-selling books with titles such as *Think and Grow Rich*. Those stories all deal with the power of expectations. If you expect to fail, your chances of succeeding are slim. Our brains don't know the difference between fantasy and reality; if you tell yourself something long enough, you will believe it. Children are even more susceptible to mental programming than adults are. If you tell a child enough times that he is stupid, he will try his best to become stupid. If you tell a child that she is smart, she will think of herself as smart and act accordingly.

In my own classrooms, I saw so many students succeed who had been labeled difficult, unteachable, slow, behaviorally disordered. I am not a miracle worker. I had no special training or equipment. What I had was the belief that all children can learn, and faith in their willingness to try.

At the start of each school year, I told each class of students: "I like you. I am glad you are in my class, and I am certain that you can earn a good grade in here. Some of the work will be hard, but you can do it if you try, and I am here to help you. I am not interested in what you have done before you came into this room. I am interested in what you do from this moment on. I expect each one of you to conduct yourself with self-respect, to work hard, and to be a responsible, successful person. I don't expect you to learn at the same rate as the person sitting next to you. If you read quickly, fine, but that doesn't make you smarter or a better person than the next student. It means you are a good reader. On the other hand, if you read slowly or poorly, it does not make you stupid or a bad person, it means you don't read very well. But you can learn. We can all learn more than we know right now, including me. I will tell you what you need to accomplish to earn an A, B, or C. You decide what grade you want to earn. The only thing that will hold you back in this class is you. You may have to work ten times harder than the person sitting next to you, but you can earn whatever grade you want in this class, if you are willing to do the work you need to do. At the end of this year, I expect everybody in this room to be a better reader, writer, and thinker than you are right now."

Those students listened and they learned. Of course, I had difficult students and a few who chose to fail, but many more students chose to believe me. My faith in them became their faith in themselves. Your attitude toward your child directly affects your child's faith—or lack of it—in him- or herself. Be careful, though, not to pretend to believe in your child's abilities. Children have built-in "b.s. detectors" and they can spot a fake in a minute. Pretending to have faith in a child doesn't help anybody, especially the child. If you have trouble believing that your child can be successful, I would ask you, Why is it impossible to believe that your child can learn? A child doesn't have to be an academic genius in order to be a healthy, happy, responsible adult who contributes to the world.

SUCCESS BREEDS SUCCESS

I have been criticized for "bribing" my students to succeed in school. I admit it. But if the offer of a candy bar, or a Friday afternoon movie in class, or a Snoopy sticker on an exam paper is what it takes to convince a child to try one time, then I'll make the bribe—because I know that once a child experiences success, bribes won't be necessary. Success feels so good that once a child feels successful, he or she will try to recapture that feeling.

You can help your child feel the glow of success by

creating a challenge or goal for your child that is possible but difficult to achieve. The task isn't as important as your encouragement and belief that your child can accomplish it. Be careful not to make it an extremely easy task, one that your child can accomplish with little effort. When the task is too easy, the child doesn't celebrate accomplishing it, if he does it at all. He may refuse even to try. Why? Because children think that we give them easy tasks because we don't think they are smart enough to accomplish "real" work. When we make things too easy, we reinforce the child's belief that she is stupid. It is much better to give a child a difficult task and help her work at it, repeating as many times as necessary in order to complete it. Completing 50 percent or 60 percent of a difficult task gives a truer sense of accomplishment and pride than completing 100 percent of a task that requires no real effort.

GET THE MESSAGE

At the risk of sounding like what my Grandpa Carl refers to as "those California touchy-feelie fruitcakes," I'd like to suggest teaching your child to use positive affirmations. (I prefer to call them positive messages.) The idea is to select a positive phrase, such as "I am wonderful," and repeat that phrase aloud, to yourself, several times each day. Little kids love them. Older kids often shrug sheepishly and hesitate, but I try to persuade them to give it a try. If they are too shy to speak out loud, I let them write the phrases in their journals. Positive messages can be just as effective if you write them down. I write them in my private journal at night before I go to sleep. At present, my positive messages include "I am a successful writer" and "I am a happy, healthy person."

Some children like to have an adult give them positive messages to repeat, others like to create their own. In my classes, I would offer several suggestions for the students who couldn't think of their own, or who wanted me to help them "get it right."

Here are some of my students' favorite sayings. I'm sure you can think of others that would suit your child:

I am a good student. I am smart. I can learn.
I am a happy, healthy, intelligent person.
I am a wonderful, lovable person.
I deserve to be successful.
I am a winner.

YOU CAN SAY THAT AGAIN

Another technique I use to plant positive thoughts in my students' minds is to hang quotations around my classroom, in the hope that when their minds wander from my lessons, they will find a positive, thought-provoking place to rest. Once in a while, somebody would question one of the quotes, or make a comment that would spark a brief discussion, so I knew they thought about them, but I didn't realize that some of them had memorized every word on those quote cards. One boy, who had

been a terror and an uninspired student as a sophomore, grew up along the way, graduated, and went off
to college. Shortly before his graduation, we met at a
football game and he asked me if I remembered the
sayings on my classroom walls. He quoted several of
them verbatim, then told me his favorite was, If your
only tool is a hammer, you tend to see every problem
as a nail.

Why not post a few positive thoughts on the walls of
your home? Or how about a quote of the week to hang
on the refrigerator door? If you have more than one child,
you might let them take turns selecting the phrase each
week. Here are some of my favorites:

- He who angers you, enslaves you.
- If you don't control your mind, somebody else will.
- I have learned tolerance from the intolerant and kind-
  ness from the unkind. I should not be ungrateful to
  those teachers.—Kahlil Gibran
- There are only two real tragedies in life. One is not
  getting your heart's desire. The other is getting it.—
  George Bernard Shaw
- One often learns more from ten days of agony than from
  ten years of contentment.—Merle Shain
- We are all given the same twenty-four hours each day.
  What you make of those hours is up to you.—Yours
  truly
- Just because you're right doesn't mean I'm wrong.—
  Alyce Johnson
- Hold fast to dreams for if dreams die, life is a broken-
  winged bird that cannot fly.—Langston Hughes

- Rudeness is a weak person's attempt at strength.— J. Matthew Casey
- The only real failure is the person who refuses to try.
- If you can imagine it, you can achieve it. If you can dream it, you can become it.—William Arthur Ward

SEND THE MESSAGE

If psychology interests you, I would recommend reading more on your own. Basic high school or college textbooks for a course such as Introduction to Psychology would be a good place to begin. (See Recommended Reading List for specific titles.) You will find some interesting theories about child and adolescent psychology. You may find yourself and your child in the pages of those texts. But a word of caution—please don't buy into the idea that there is a "normal" time line for a child to develop. Every child has a built-in, personal time line for mental, physical, and emotional development. Some of the smartest, most successful people in the world have been labeled failures in school. Fortunately, they didn't let other people's opinions stop them from succeeding. But for every child who refuses to let other people define him, there are thousands who never recover from their school days. They start out behind the pack, or fall behind, and never get over the feeling that they aren't smart enough or good enough. They spend their lives feeling as though there is something wrong with them.

On the other hand, if we treat children with dignity and respect and give them unconditional love and acceptance, and if we truly believe that they can achieve, they will carry that message with them for the rest of their lives. You can do much to help your child succeed in school, and in life, by sending a clear message: *You can learn it; you can do it; you can become it. Try.*

Chapter 9

TROUBLESHOOTING

You are certain that your child has good vision and hearing, but his grades are poor. The next question to ask is, *Does my child sincerely want to succeed in school?* If the answer is "Yes," if your child's attendance, behavior, and attitude are good in spite of bad grades, I would suggest that you arrange to have your child tested for learning disabilities.

DISABILITY DOESN'T MEAN DUMB

Sometimes, parents are reluctant to have their children tested because they think they will be blamed for the condition, but educators are interested in helping children learn, not in placing blame. Many parents fear that a learning disability indicates a low IQ, but *a learning disability is* not *a sign of low intelligence.* I can't repeat that often enough. I wish I could write it in the sky for all of the people who suffer in silence because they can't spell or read or pronounce words perfectly.

Think of a learning disability as a short circuit. A signal is being misrouted or misinterpreted somewhere along the line, and it causes problems in processing, interpreting, or articulating information. With dyslexia, for example, a student may look at the word *pop* and see *bob* or *dod*— or something entirely different—because a glitch occurs somewhere between the eyes and the brain. With other processing disorders, sounds may enter the student's ear but become distorted before the brain can process them, or a student may be thinking of a particular word but find himself unable to say it out loud.

A learning disability doesn't necessarily prevent a student from understanding information—some of the brightest students I've ever had were severely dyslexic. One boy in my junior English class, Joe, could not spell the simplest words or write a legible sentence, but during an independent reading project, he read three novels (including *The Hobbit,* which is not easy reading) while the other students in his class read one, and he single-handedly prepared and presented to the class his group's analysis and comparisons of the books they had read.

Some students learn to cope with disabilities very well. In fact, sometimes they learn to cope so well that other people have trouble believing their success. Joe's mother arrived at my doorstep shortly after Joe's first semester report card had arrived in her mailbox. I overheard Joe and his mother outside my classroom, arguing in whispers. "Mom, you're embarrassing me," Joe said. "I earned my grade. Honest." He stayed in the hallway while his mother came in to talk to me. She introduced herself and asked me how in the world Joe could have earned an A in English.

"Do you mean because he can't spell?" I asked. She nodded. I explained that I didn't require Joe to take spelling tests, and that he took some of his other exams orally. I explained that I didn't give him spelling tests for the same reason I wouldn't ask a child with one leg to run a foot race. It would set him up to fail. I also explained that her son knew how to think, how to articulate his thoughts grammatically and intelligently, and that he was a conscientious worker who knew how to set priorities and always turned in his assignments. He never cut class and was never late. In my opinion, he was not only an A student, but an A person. She then asked me whether I had noticed Joe's attention problem.

"Excuse me?" I said, thinking I had misunderstood.

"Joe suffers from Attention Deficit Disorder," his mother said.

"Not in my class, he doesn't," I said. "He's always on task and sometimes spends the entire fifty-minute class period working on one assignment. Are you sure he has ADD?"

"Well, he stopped taking his medication this year," Joe's mother said, "and I was afraid it would have a negative effect on his work. He said he didn't need to take it." She was silent for a moment. "Maybe he was right."

Maybe he was, or maybe he didn't like being labeled. Which brings me to the next point. I'm prepared to hear some protests from parents and educational diagnosticians, but I am willing to risk those protests on behalf of the many children who hate being labeled, who have been mistakenly labeled, and who have been taught to use their labels as crutches or excuses. Please understand that I realize some children honestly do have disabilities and need special help, but I think it's important for us to realize that some children have serious troubles because they have serious difficulties in their personal lives, they suffer from food allergies or inadequate diet, or they simply don't fit the mold that our school system dictates. I have had many children in my classes who were labeled as having Attention Deficit Disorder or Behavior Disorder or some other term but who performed well, did the work, and honestly earned their good grades.

Sometimes I wonder whether we shouldn't just lump all of the children who have troubles into one group and label them DDWWWWWWTT—Don't Do What We Want When We Want Them To. For goodness sake, doesn't it make sense that some students, especially small children, find it difficult to sit in a hard wooden or plastic chair for long periods of time and perform tasks that are mentally exhausting? Recently, while thumbing through some old educational journals, I read a report (*Educational Leadership*, March 1987) about research on student learning that said the typical school chair forces 75 percent of the student's body weight to be supported by only 4 square inches of bone. Classroom chairs haven't changed much during the past ten years, so is it any wonder that some children constantly wiggle and jiggle and have trouble staying in their seats? Older students often try to alleviate the pain by disrupting class and being sent to the office.

For them, the reprimand is worth the chance to move freely and stretch their aching bodies.

B.D.

Last year, I had a freshman in my first period English class who had been classified as Behavior Disordered and spent most of his day in a special classroom. Three periods per day, he was permitted to attend "regular" classes like mine. I was not notified of Lino's B.D. classification (not an unusual practice in public schools). For the first week of classes, Lino was a model student. In fact, he completed most of the assignments ahead of the class and earned high grades on them. Then one morning as I was seated amidst the students, hoping my participation and modeling would motivate them to work harder, Lino reached up from behind, grabbed a handful of my hair, and gave it a good yank. I whirled around and grabbed Lino's hand in midair.

"What's wrong with you?" I shouted, angry because my head still hurt.

"I'm B.D.," Lino said simply, as though that excused his behavior.

"I don't care what you are," I said. "You know how to behave. I've seen you do it for a whole week. So don't tell me you can't behave. You can if you want to, and you will if you want to remain in this class. If you can't behave, then you can go back to the special classroom and act however you please. I hope you decide to behave yourself because I like you and I think you're pretty sharp, but it's up to you."

Lino chose to remain in my class and behave himself. He mentioned the incident to his counselor, who asked me if his behavior had improved. When I told her that I occasionally had to remind Lino to settle down, but that we'd had no serious problems, she was clearly surprised. She told me that he had been removed from his two other regular classes for causing too many disruptions.

I'm not saying I'm a better teacher than those other two, or that Lino didn't have a problem controlling himself. What I'm saying is that I think we need to be very careful that we don't give students permission to misbehave by telling them that it isn't their fault, so they don't have to accept responsibility for their actions. I think we need to hold them more responsible for their behavior, but we must also provide clear guidelines and help them develop self-discipline and control while we try to discover the reasons for their behavior. Many of my students who have been labeled B.D. were very angry or very scared, sometimes both, and usually with good reason. I think we would make better use of our time and energy if, instead of labeling children and separating them from others, we tried to help them learn to cope with their anger and fear so they could fit in.

SUGAR HIGH

There is another contributor to student attention problems that needs to be addressed: sugar high. Ask any classroom teacher to compare student behavior before and after lunch hour at a school where students have free access to soda and snack machines. Yes, schools do provide nutritional lunches for students, but when students have the option of eating a hot meal or snacking on chips, sodas, and candy, most of them go for the quick fix. The difference in behavior is easy to see. After munching on candy bars and sugary drinks (many of which are also high in caffeine), students are easily distracted and much more prone to disruptive behavior. As one teacher friend put it, "I hate fifth period because I have to keep scraping the kids off the ceiling."

I have been present at staff meetings when teachers have requested that the snack machines either be removed or replaced with machines offering healthier alternatives such as yogurt, fruit, pretzels, sandwiches, or individual containers of soup or stew, and that drink machines include fruit juices and bottled water. Even when administrators agree with the teachers, the snack machines stay and the subject is forgotten. Why? Economics, apathy, resistance to change, contracts with snack companies, lack of statistics to support the change, and so on and so forth. Perhaps if parents joined with teachers to request healthy alternatives, or at least limited access to snack machines, we might be able to make some changes. I honestly believe that if we eliminated or reduced the sugar and caffeine consumption of our schoolchildren, we would see not only better behavior and grades, but a significant reduction in the number of students diagnosed as learning disabled or behavior disordered.

LABEL WITH CARE

When we label children as anything, gifted or challenged, we define part of their personality and limit their freedom to develop as people because they accept our definitions of them. I've seen gifted children who thrived on the pressure and constant challenge of accelerated classes, but I have also seen gifted children who were mentally and emotionally exhausted by the time they reached their final years of high school because they had been pushed to the very limit of their abilities or restricted to the most difficult academic classes and never permitted to study any subject for the pure joy of learning.

Even more devastating and heartbreaking than seeing students who have been pushed too hard is seeing students who have been held back all their lives. In my own classroom, I had a student who had been placed in special education classes all of her life after being diagnosed as mentally retarded. Nobody, including Amanda, had ever questioned the diagnosis until she applied for permission to enter the Academy program at our school. The other teachers and I voted to accept Amanda because of her pleasant personality, her willingness to work hard, and her passing grades in every subject. After a year in the program, Amanda suddenly began to make amazing progress in every subject, and her grades improved dramatically. One day, she wrote in her journal, "I just finished reading a book for the first time in my life. I read a whole book. It's totally cool. Now I'm going to read all the books I want."

Unfortunately, Amanda's parents couldn't believe what had happened. They thought we were giving Amanda high grades because we liked her. Although we assured them that Amanda was doing the same work as the other children, they couldn't accept the truth, and removed her from the program. Shortly thereafter, Amanda was sent to a different school and we lost touch. Three years later, a young woman appeared in my classroom one afternoon as I was about to leave school. It was Amanda. I didn't recognize her until she spoke because she looked so different. Instead of a shy, self-conscious adolescent, I was facing a self-assured young woman.

"I just wanted you to know that I'm in college now," Amanda told me, "and I'm studying to be a special education teacher. I'm going to help kids who have problems in school."

Amanda is not the only one. I'm sure you've heard stories. Les Brown, the renowned motivational speaker, was diagnosed as educable mentally retarded as a child and was placed in special classes until high school, when a teacher recognized his intelligence and ability and told him to stop letting people label him. On one episode of the television program *60 Minutes*, one of the students of noted teacher and author Marva Collins recalls being told as a child that she would never be able to learn. Not so long ago, that child, now a grown woman, graduated from college summa cum laude and is preparing to enter law school. Unfortunately, there are many more examples. I'm not telling you to disregard the experts, or refuse to accept help if your child needs it, but I am asking you to give your child the benefit of the doubt before you decide what he can or cannot learn.

Let me reiterate that I do believe there are some children who have severe problems trying to process information or controlling their behavior, and those children do need special help. It's important for children with true learning disabilities to be tested and diagnosed so that they can receive assistance, but also so that they can learn to cope or compensate for their problems. It's even more important that students with problems that might prevent them from completing graduation requirements be tested and diagnosed so that they can apply for waivers where applicable. Two of my students in California had processing disorders that prevented them from passing one of the four written exams required for graduation. Both boys were bright students and hard workers. With waivers, they were able to complete extra courses, with one-on-one help from a special education teacher, that took the place of the exams, and both boys received their high school diplomas. Without the waivers, they would have been denied their diplomas even though they had successfully completed twelve years of classes.

HOW CAN YOU TELL?

Your child's teachers are probably the best source of information about your child's performance, but there are things you can watch for at home if you suspect a learning disorder. Children who have to point at every single word while reading or they lose their place; children who can't spell anything, no matter how hard they try; children who squint or hold books very close to their faces or who sit very close to the television; children who frequently confuse sounds; children who complain of frequent headaches or whose eyes ache and water when they read; children who hold books upside down when they read or who prefer to read in very dim light; children who can't seem to remember verbal instructions; children who refuse to write anything at all; children who cannot get along with other children under any circumstances; children who refuse to speak. Any of the above behaviors might be seen in any child on a given day, but if you recognize several of them, or see them frequently, it could be an indication that testing is in order.

CAN'T—OR WON'T?

Misbehavior is so rampant that I have heard teachers joke that out of thirty-five students in a class, all but two have been diagnosed as behavior disordered, and those two are absent four out of five days. Sometimes I wonder whether we don't have unreasonable expectations of our students today. Yes, I went to school when students sat in their seats, kept their mouths shut, raised their hands for permission to speak, and accepted every word a teacher said as the law. If we didn't do those things, we were paddled by the teacher, paddled again by the principal, and once again for good measure when we got home. Is it any wonder that we behaved well?

If your child misbehaves frequently in school, he may suffer from a behavioral or emotional disorder that he cannot control. Or he may be bored, crying for attention, or simply trying to see whether he can upset the teacher because it amuses him.

Your child may be using bad behavior and poor grades to manipulate or punish somebody (including himself) or to express anger or fear. A negative or apathetic attitude is quite often a childish attempt to hide insecurity. The simplest way to find out whether your child needs "an attitude check" is to ask your child if she wants to succeed in school. If the answer is "I don't know" or "I don't care," the real answer is probably closer to, "I don't think I can succeed, so I'm not going to try" or "I'm going to pretend I don't care because I'm afraid that I can't succeed." Students who lack motivation often receive stern lectures and warnings when what they need is a boost in self-confidence and self-esteem. No, I'm not suggesting that we excuse their bad behavior, but that we try to understand it so we can change it.

Think about it—do you honestly believe that your child wants to fail or truly doesn't care if he does fail? If so, you face the difficult task of figuring out why, and you'll probably need more help than I can offer in these few pages. You might start with the school psychologist or counselor and ask him or her to help you determine the best course of action.

If you don't believe your child wants to fail but is afraid that she can't succeed, you can help her overcome her fear of trying by reminding her that everybody, including you, is afraid sometimes, but that it is far better to try and fail than never to try at all. Share some of your own childhood experiences about times when you were afraid or when you failed, and how you coped with those failures. Better yet, try something new and difficult, along with your child, and keep trying until you achieve some measure of success. Draw a picture of your dog or try to climb a rope or get a videotape and take a dance lesson in your living room. Whip out a cookbook and try to bake a fluffy soufflé, see if you can stand on your head for a full minute (in your backyard, if you're shy), or buy a bow and arrow and practice target shooting. What you try doesn't matter—the point is to let your child see you trying something new. Don't give up too soon, but don't push yourself too hard trying to be perfect—teach your child by example that it's all right not to be perfect, that there is pleasure in testing your own limits, even when you don't succeed.

MY CHILD WOULD NEVER DO SUCH A THING!

Maybe not while you're looking, but you'd be surprised what kids will do when you aren't around. And it isn't a reflection on you. If a teacher calls to tell you that your child has said or done something naughty or terrible or downright disgusting, don't panic. If you immediately deny that your child did or said this thing, it may put the teacher on the defensive and he or she may feel compelled to prove that your child is at fault. Instead, ask the teacher to explain exactly what happened. Then, discuss the incident with your child before deciding what consequences or punishment to assign. Sometimes the teacher doesn't have all the facts. Kids are very good at placing blame on other people, and they hate to "rat" on the guilty party, even if it means they take somebody else's lumps.

What if a teacher insists that your child is guilty, but you believe he's innocent? Tell the teacher you will handle the matter at home. Be careful that you don't give the impression to your child that you will always take his side against a teacher. But do make it clear that you trust your child and will continue to do so as long as you are convinced that he is honest with you.

What if it turns out that the teacher is right and your child really did do this terrible thing? Of course, appropriate consequences need to be assigned—but I think it's just as important to find out *why* a child does something, and to insist that the child accept responsibility, as it is to punish him for it. Punishment isn't very effective in preventing misbehavior because children focus on the embarrassment, pain, or anger the punishment causes, instead of taking responsibility for their behavior and learning to act more appropriately.

Children don't have our experience and background to draw upon when they have to make decisions, so they do some strange things. What appears to us to be bad or wrong behavior may not seem that way to a young person. Here are two examples from my own classroom that made me realize the importance of understanding the reason for a student's behavior.

"I Was Just Gonna Stick the Gun in His Face." Manny, a wiry little fellow about five feet tall, brought a handgun (unloaded) to school one day and put it in his locker. Manny wasn't a violent boy. If he hadn't told me himself, I wouldn't have believed he'd brought the gun. I knew his parents, and I am sure they would have been shocked, too. Manny brought the gun to school because a bigger boy kept beating him up, and Manny couldn't think of any other defense. Fortunately, he wrote about

the gun in his private journal, and I was able to persuade him to get rid of it before he showed it to anybody else.

"The gun wasn't loaded," Manny told me, "but he doesn't know that. I was just going to stick it in his face and tell him to leave me alone or I'd blow his brains out."

After Manny got rid of the gun, we sat down to talk. At first, he insisted that his solution was the only one that would work; the bully wouldn't understand anything except the threat of a bullet. I argued that there must be other possible solutions, but I couldn't come up with any. Telling his parents or the principal wouldn't work because the bully had a lot of big friends, and Manny was certain they would hurt him worse if he turned them in. I hated to admit it, but I agreed with Manny. We talked for quite a long time and finally decided that we should ask the other students in Manny's class for some suggestions.

Several husky football players in the class volunteered to hold a brief discussion with the bully in question. They explained to him that they did not appreciate him picking on their classmate and would like him to stop immediately. He did. It wasn't a solution I would have suggested, but it worked. (No, I *don't* condone violence—the boys gave me their word of honor that there would be no hitting, just very loud talking.)

Manny was lucky. If a security guard had found the gun, Manny would have been expelled and labeled a violent delinquent. He would have been sent to juvenile hall, where he would probably have learned many things we would rather he didn't know, but he wouldn't have learned how to deal with bullies in a nonviolent, lawful way. What might have turned out to be a tragic incident for Manny turned out to be a very good lesson for both him and me. I learned to keep my mouth shut and listen before assuming that I know why somebody has done a particular thing. Manny learned that there are alternative solutions to any problem, and sometimes the good guys really do win.

"I Just Know My Mama Will Kill Me." Genna stopped me in the hallway after school. "Miss Johnson, I gotta talk to you," she whispered. "This is a matter of life or death and I'm serious."

We went to a quiet corner to talk and Genna explained that she had spent all night at school, hiding in an empty classroom. She was afraid to go home and face her mother because she had been lying for weeks about her grades. When her interim report card had shown two D's, Genna had convinced her mother that the grades were an error, that they were actually B's. Genna thought she could bring up the grades before the end of the term, but she hadn't been able to do it. She had fallen too far behind in advanced math and Spanish to make up the work. Her final report card showed two D's and it was due to arrive in the mail that day.

"I can't go home and face my mama," Genna said. "I know her. She will beat me so bad and then she'll kick me out of the house. Not because of my grades so much, but because I lied to her. She made me promise one time never to lie to her, and I never did until now." I told Genna I thought she might be underestimating her mother. Genna insisted that I was the one who underestimated her mother. Genna's mother had had to drop out of high school to raise Genna, and she was determined that her daughter was going to finish high school and go on to college. "She doesn't want me to have a hard life like she did," Genna told me, big tears rolling down her cheeks. "She is so strict with me, but she really loves me and now look what I went and did. She's going to kill me for lying and getting bad grades and now she'll kill me worse because I ran away, too."

I offered to go home with her, but Genna said it would only make her mother more furious if somebody else knew their personal business. I suggested that she call her mother first, but Genna refused, saying a phone call would give her mother time to work up a really good fit of anger before she got home.

"Then why don't you write your mother a letter," I suggested. "Tell her you are sorry you lied to her, that you never lied to her before and you will never do it again. Ask her to forgive you. Explain that you were ashamed. You didn't want her to be disappointed in you, and you thought you could bring up those grades. Then tell her that you realize it was a mistake, that you love her very much, and you realize that she is so strict with you because she loves you and wants to help you. Tell her you are going to be home in one hour. Send somebody else to deliver your letter, then go home and take the consequences. Since you have a good relationship with your mother, and you know she loves you, I think you should trust her not to beat you or kick you out of the house. If she does, you call me and we'll think of something to do."

Genna's mother didn't beat her or kick her out of the house. She cried and hugged her daughter and told her she was sorry she had placed so much pressure on her.

She also said it was a good thing that Genna had written the letter, because it gave her time to calm down before they talked. She had already called the police to report Genna's disappearance and the office to complain about what she thought were errors on Genna's report card. She admitted that she would have been too angry to listen to any excuses if Genna had been home when the report card arrived.

She didn't punish Genna for lying, but she canceled Genna's summer vacation visit to her grandmother's house so Genna could retake both courses in summer school. And she made it clear that she expected Genna to tell her the next time she had a problem, and not make up a lie to avoid facing the consequences.

IT'S EASY FOR ME TO SAY

Perhaps you're reading this and thinking, "Ha! It's easy for her to tell me to be calm and listen to my children before I fly off the handle and punish them. She doesn't have to put up with them twenty-four hours a day and pay for the damage they do and worry about them getting themselves pregnant or arrested or killed."

If that's what you're thinking, I won't argue. You're absolutely right. Teaching is a difficult job, but it isn't nearly as hard as yours. Good luck.

CHANGING THE SUBJECT

Perhaps your child isn't responsible for her problems at school; perhaps she has good vision and hearing, lots of motivation, good thinking skills, and excellent study habits. In that case, we need to consider the subject matter and the teacher. I'll save the best for last and talk about subject matter now.

I don't know which is worse—a class that is too hard for a student, or one that is too easy. In either case, students have difficulty paying attention, they lack the motivation to complete assignments, and they find it difficult to resist the temptation to misbehave. In a perfect world, a student who was insufficiently challenged would simply be moved to a more challenging class. In the real world, that option doesn't always exist, so we need to find alternative solutions. If your child complains that a class is too easy, and you are convinced that this is true, by all means, ask about the possibility of a change. A note of caution here. I have had students who insisted that the assignments were too easy, when they didn't have a clue about the concepts involved. They didn't realize that they didn't understand the assignments well enough to do them properly. But if you're certain . . .

If a change to a more challenging class isn't possible, or your child doesn't want to move ahead without his classmates (some kids hate to be accelerated), there are still several good options. Your child could take a book to class and read until the bell rings if he finishes his work early. He could do homework from other classes, request additional assignments (for fun or credit), read ahead in the text, ask for permission to work on the next assignment, volunteer to tutor other students, assist the teacher by grading papers or delivering items to the office. If the teacher disagrees with all of these suggestions, I would try to change classes (or teacher, if the student stays in the same classroom all day). Students should not be expected to sit and twiddle their thumbs until the bell rings.

A class may be too difficult for your child for a variety of reasons. Sometimes a student is ill or distracted during key lessons and may need remedial work to catch up to the other students. Some subjects, such as math, build upon previous knowledge, with each year's lessons serving as building blocks for the following year. If a student misses one or more of those building blocks, he may not be able to progress in the subject without going back and relearning the missing information.

Before you remove your child from a class because it's too difficult, I would recommend remedial help—at home, at school, or both. If remedial work doesn't help, and your child is honestly trying, it could be that your child's brain simply isn't ready for the level of understanding required. There is a point at which a child's brain makes the switch from concrete to abstract thinking. Concrete thinking means two plus two is four: *I can see the four objects, so this concept makes sense to me.* Abstract thinking requires understanding of things that cannot be touched or photographed or visualized. Symbolism, for example, is an abstract concept that freshman students are expected to understand. In literature, a bird singing sweetly may symbolize happiness or love, but to a child who can't think in abstractions, a bird singing is the sound of a bird singing and nothing else.

There is no "normal" age at which a child's brain

makes the switch to abstract thinking capability, and it isn't obvious to us when that switch occurs. But I think many problems, particularly in mathematics, occur because we expect children to do things that they simply aren't ready to do. Even the most brilliant child will fail if her brain hasn't developed enough to handle the thoughts we're asking her to consider.

Imagine how you would feel if you were expected to be able to do everything that other people your age (whether you're thirty or fifty-seven or ninety-two) could do—and do all equally well. It sounds ridiculous, but that's what we do to children in our age-based school system. From the first day they enter a classroom, our children are expected to learn at the same rate as the other children of a specific age, and I think this is the root of many problems that persist for years, sometimes long after students leave high school. Unfortunately, many students, not just young ones, perceive their places in the world and their comparative worth as people based on how well they compare to the other students in their classrooms. It doesn't fool children for a minute if you name their reading groups the Bluebirds and the Robins to avoid labeling them according to their abilities (which in school is so often interpreted as intelligence), the kids know exactly where they fall in the ranks of their class.

Competition is good, you might argue, because it encourages people to strive to achieve goals. Perhaps it does, when people believe they have a chance of succeeding, but I don't think competition or constant comparison motivates young students and I don't think it's fair. In fact, sometimes it's downright stupid. For example, as I mentioned in a previous chapter, I had two students in the same sophomore English class—one who sported a full beard and the thickened body of a grown man, the other a short, skinny boy who was all elbows and knees and still had the soft pink face of a baby. The smaller boy was the older of the two. I can't imagine how anybody could have expected those two boys to learn at the same rate, given the extreme difference in their physical development, yet we make those expectations all the time in our age-based school system. During school, the ones who are advanced spend twelve years feeling superior and the ones who are behind spend those same years feeling inferior. Some people never get over those feelings—I know, because they write me letters from all over the country.

Diane, a forty-one-year-old woman from West Virginia, wrote to tell me about her eighth-grade teacher's response to an essay assignment. The assignment had been for students to write their opinions on a particular topic. Here is an excerpt from her letter:

I do not remember the subject or how I responded. However, I do remember the teacher practically snickering, the red F for failure, and the comment, 'this is not the correct answer' written at the top of the page. When I questioned the grade, reiterating the fact that she wanted my opinion, she just laughed and said she felt I was wrong: therefore, I deserved an F . . . (I just learned in the past three years that my opinion is valuable and I am worth something.)

. . . Just wanted you to know—this is not a pity story— I've managed to become a hard-working, dedicated, loyal employee, in spite of, not because of my teachers.

After reading *My Posse Don't Do Homework*, Lindsey, a fifteen-year-old high school freshman from New Mexico, wrote to tell me about her school experience.

> I personally have had the privilege of growing up in a strong family environment and have not experienced many of the educational obstacles that the characters in your story have gone through. . . . I am a child of a middle class family and am currently attending a prestigious Catholic high school. . . . From past experiences of being "left in the dust" when I didn't quite catch onto something, I really could've used a teacher . . . who was able to listen to my personal needs as an individual student, and most importantly as an individual person who makes mistakes.

The feeling of being "left in the dust" isn't necessarily a byproduct of overcrowded public schools, as Lindsey points out. Unfortunately, there are many, many Dianes and Lindseys in our public and private schools because most of our elementary and secondary schools are designed for ease of administration. When you group children solely by age, you know exactly how many students will be in each classroom. If you grouped them by ability and readiness to move forward, it would require more time and energy because you would actually have to spend time with them individually. That's what keeps us from changing our school system to fit the needs of students instead of the needs of the adults who work within the system. It takes too much time, and time is the one thing we deny our children, unless they cause such problems that they force us to address their needs.

A reporter recently asked me how I would respond to

the claim that by establishing so many alternative and charter schools we are rewarding students for misbehaving. My response? I believe the growing number of alternative schools indicates that our children are demanding the schools we should have given them in the first place—smaller schools with fewer students per classroom, individual attention from teachers, recognition of their personal needs and learning rates, and flexibility to work around the obstacles presented by their difficult lives.

Okay, I'll climb down off my soapbox now and talk about teachers.

THE TEACHER-STUDENT CONNECTION

If your child performs poorly in one teacher's class, but well in others, it may be the subject matter (math is easy, but English is difficult), the time of day (lots of kids flake out after lunch or run out of gas at 2:00 P.M.)—or it may be the teacher. Many teacher-student problems occur because students don't know how to talk to adults, are afraid of them, or resent their authority. Students need to approach their teachers with the same tact and diplomacy with which we approach our supervisors at work. For example, if a student wants to discuss a grade that he thinks is incorrect, the teacher isn't going to be receptive to holding a discussion in the few brief minutes directly before or after class begins, just as your boss would probably not appreciate coming to work to find you waiting on her doorstep with a complaint about your salary. "When could I come and talk to you about my grade?"

is much more likely to result in a productive conversation than, "Hey, you made a mistake. You got my grade wrong."

Nobody likes to have his authority challenged, and it's human nature to feel attacked when somebody questions the accuracy or quality of our work. If the student immediately claims that the teacher is wrong, the teacher is very apt to feel insulted and compelled to try to prove that he or she computed the grade correctly. By using a little tact, students can avoid putting the teacher on the defensive. Here are some of the suggestions I give my own students to help them learn to talk to other teachers:

"I'd really like to earn a B in this class. Could you tell me what I need to do to bring up my grade?"

"I thought I was doing better than the grade on my report card. Could you show me why I got this grade and help me figure out how to raise it?"

"I've been trying to keep track of my grades and I got a different percentage than you did. Could you show me where I made a mistake?"

When one of my students wants to change classes because of problems with the teacher, I try to discourage the student. First, there is no guarantee that the next teacher will be better, and the nicest teacher isn't always the best teacher. Some of my most unlikable teachers gave me the best education. Second, I don't want to encourage my students to run away from their problems or think that I (or some other adult) will always be able to rescue them from painful situations. I ask them to sit down with me and try to figure out if there is any way they can resolve the problem without changing the class. Sometimes the solution is simple: Talk to the teacher.

NO ENTIENDO

Two of my best students, both native Spanish speakers, kept getting in trouble for speaking Spanish during their math class.

"The teacher gets so mad," Maria said, "and we aren't doing anything wrong. It's just that sometimes we don't understand the problem in English, so we tell each other how to say it in Spanish and then we can do it."

I suggested that they tell their math teacher what they had just told me. They were skeptical, but agreed to give it a try. The following day, they reported that Mr. Banks thanked them for taking the time to talk to him. He said it hadn't occurred to him that they might need help in translating the problems, since they were such intelligent young ladies. He had been more concerned that they do their own work so they would learn the material.

SHE HATES ME

Another student, Derrick, complained that his French teacher didn't like him because his handwriting was illegible. "She hates me," Derrick complained. "She won't grade my papers, even when I have all the answers right. She just gives me a zero because she says she can't read my writing." I asked Derrick if other teachers had complained about the same problem.

"Yeah," he admitted. "Ever since I was in first grade. All my teachers complain about my writing being sloppy. I've tried to make it better, but it doesn't work.

Sometimes I copy my papers over twice, but they don't look any better."

I suggested that Derrick ask if his French teacher would accept typewritten papers. Derrick protested, saying it would be more work, and would require a lot more time, to type his papers. And besides, he didn't have a typewriter or a computer at home.

"Don't you want to pass this class?" I asked him. "Isn't it worth your time and effort to earn the credit? And what about the teacher? She has to read thirty papers from each class. You only have to write one paper—so she's still doing more work than you are." I told him he could use my computer, or we'd ask the business teacher for permission to use a typewriter during lunch or after school.

Derrick agreed and made arrangements to use my computer during lunchtimes and after school to type his papers. He said his parents promised to buy him a computer if he passed the class with a C or higher. He earned an A in the class and decided that maybe his French teacher liked him after all.

I know I sound like Pollyana sometimes, but very often the solution is so simple that we overlook it. Sometimes all we have to do is talk to each other. And listen.

In those two examples, the teacher-student relationship was improved through communication or patience. Sometimes, though, the only logical solution is to request a transfer. Most administrators will cooperate if you request a transfer for your child because you honestly believe that a teacher has a personal dislike for your child or is unable to teach him effectively for some legitimate reason. But if you make a habit of demanding different teachers, you run the risk of being labeled as a "problem parent," and the staff of your school will become much less willing to work with you. If you try to run interference every time your child has a problem at school, your child will be the one who suffers. I think it would be better to try to help your child develop problem-solving and personal interaction skills.

The Case of the Crabby Computer Teacher   Unlike Derrick's case, where his teacher's complaint was perfectly valid, another student, Punky, came to me for advice when his computer teacher decided to use him as a scapegoat for the entire class. Nearly every day, Mr. Tinker ordered Punky out of the room, to the office, or to detention.

"He makes up all kinds of cheesy excuses just because he doesn't like me," Punky insisted. Other students in the class confirmed Punky's story. Mr. Tinker really did seem to be picking on Punky, they said. Sometimes five or six students would be reprimanded for talking during class, but Punky was the only one Mr. Tinker punished.

(I'd like to point out that I don't make a habit of discussing other teachers with my students, and I don't always assume that my students are perfect angels, but in this case, the teacher had a reputation as being unpleasant to staff and students alike. If you asked anybody on campus to describe Mr. Tinker in one word, I think the odds are very good that the person would say, "crabby.")

Punky wanted to drop Mr. Tinker's computer course immediately, but I convinced him to give it some time before he insisted on changing the class, because the content of the course was important and valuable.

"But he sends me to the principal's office every day for

stupid little stuff like I forgot to bring a pencil, or my book was open to the wrong page," Punky argued.

"Then I would bet that the principal is going to get tired of handling Mr. Tinker's trivial problems," I said. "Just wait a few more weeks and see."

"But what about me?" Punky asked. "My mom's going to get really mad if I keep getting sent to the office every day because they call her up and tell on me."

I offered to call Punky's mother and explain that I believed Punky was being unfairly punished, but that I didn't think the problem would last much longer. She thanked me for assuring her that Punky hadn't turned into a juvenile delinquent and agreed to wait until I called her before she took any action.

"If Mr. Tinker sends you to the office, you go," I told Punky. "And you be very polite. Just go and sit in the hallway and be respectful when the principal calls you in. The only way he is going to believe that Mr. Tinker is picking on you is if you let him see for himself." I also warned Punky that if I found out he was doing anything at all to antagonize Mr. Tinker, or that he had talked about the situation with other kids, he would be in big trouble with me and the principal. I didn't want him to create bad morale in Mr. Tinker's class or turn other students against the teacher. Punky promised to keep his mouth shut and his nose clean.

It worked. After about two weeks, Punky's daily visits to the office stopped. When I asked a staff secretary if she knew anything about the situation, she confided that the principal had sent a memo to Mr. Tinker requesting that he try harder to maintain order in his classroom, and that he send only severe behavior problems to the office.

Teacher from Another Planet If your own experience in school was anything like mine, you had some teachers who were good at their jobs and nice people, too. But I swear I had some teachers who lived in caves and sprouted fangs during a full moon. Like any other profession, teaching has its good and bad, with a few greats and a handful of terribles. Regardless of their training, teachers tend to follow their own teachers' examples. We have veteran teachers who attended schools when paddlings and knuckle cracking were common; those teachers expect blind obedience and often have a difficult time handling the questioning attitude of today's young people. And, unfortunately, many teachers grew up at a time when non-English-speaking Americans were discouraged from teaching their children the family's native language (before we realized that children can learn two languages at a time). Those are the teachers who become upset when children speak anything except English in class.

And, let's face it. Some teachers can be cruel. Some are prejudiced. Some are chauvinistic. Some are intolerant of any religion or lifestyle that is different from their own. Some are simply obnoxious. In a different situation, personality and character might not be so important, but the personalities and attitudes of teachers can affect other people's lives, sometimes permanently.

Arm Your Child Against Prejudice Prejudice in the classroom isn't limited to religion, gender, race, or skin color. A child's weight, intelligence, attractiveness, and social skills can also be the source of bias. Once, a teacher actually told me, "I never give a fat girl an A." He said he was ashamed of himself, but that didn't excuse him, and it didn't help the girls in his classes. I don't think most teachers are as aware of their prejudices as that teacher was, but I know that they do exist because I have experienced them from the other side of the desk during my own school days. I try to help my students understand that it is the prejudiced person who has the true problem. Society is filled with people who hold every kind of bias imaginable, so it is impossible to protect our children against prejudice and the pain it produces. But we can teach them to value themselves, to understand that prejudice is a sign of ignorance and fear, not a reflection of their personal worth. If you can't remove your child from an environment in which he or she faces prejudice, then you can use it as an opportunity to help your child develop the strength of character to ignore the prejudice and use it as motivation to work harder and succeed in spite of other people's ignorance and cruelty. As Eleanor Roosevelt said, "Nobody can make you feel inferior without your consent."

When the Teacher Is the Problem   If you have explored every other possibility and now suspect that your child's problem is the teacher, don't automatically take sides, but do make it clear to your child that you want to help him solve this problem. Ask your child to explain his point of view. Next, I would suggest going directly to the source and asking the teacher to assess the situation. Be tactful, but straightforward. You might open the conversation by saying something such as, "I realize that Sherry sometimes has a stubborn personality," or "At home, James often has a negative attitude. Is that causing a problem in your class?" Admitting that you realize your child isn't perfect may encourage the teacher to admit that he or she isn't perfect, either.

Perhaps you will realize, after talking to the teacher, that there is a conflict in learning-teaching styles. Your child may learn by seeing or doing, for example, and the teacher may rely primarily on lecturing during lessons. In that case, your child might simply need to learn how to ask for help (see Chapter 7).

If you talk to your child and the teacher, and you still aren't sure what is happening in the classroom, I would ask other children—classmates, brothers and sisters, neighbors, friends—what they know about this particular teacher's personality and reputation. Call the guidance counselor at school and ask whether the teacher is known to have trouble handling specific student behaviors. Don't accuse the teacher of being difficult, but explain that you are trying to understand why your child is having problems in the teacher's class. (Be prepared: Some counselors will talk freely, others will try to brush you off. In school districts where there has been a lot of conflict between teachers and administrators, staff may be instructed not to discuss anything except recorded grades, absences, and so on.)

After you've gotten as much information as you can from different sources, if you honestly believe that your child's teacher is the real problem, you have a difficult decision to make. Should you tell your child that although you realize this teacher is difficult, he can't run from his problems and he needs to learn to deal with the teacher? Or should you insist that your child be transferred to another class? If a teacher simply has a difficult personality, a contrary nature, or an overly strict approach to teaching,

I would think twice before assuming that your child will suffer from being in the teacher's class. It might turn out to be a good experience in the long run. I would suggest helping your child learn to cope with a difficult situation, unless you believe it will cause permanent emotional damage or will result in the child being prevented from moving to the next grade or graduating on time.

When a student complains to me about another teacher being mean, too strict, unfair, or too picky, I say, "Learn how to deal with this person. It will be good practice for your future. If you go to college, you are bound to find some impossible professors. And unless you are unusually lucky, you are going to have a boss someday who will drive you crazy. Then there is the possibility that your future mother-in-law or father-in-law may be a prickly pear. Your next-door neighbor might not like your politics. The sooner you learn to deal with difficult or nasty or prejudiced people, the easier the rest of your life will be. Life isn't fair and some things are worth fighting for or against. But choose your battles carefully so you don't waste your time and energy unless it's really necessary and important to you. Then, when you do choose to fight, use your brain."

Chapter 10

DRUGS, DRINKING, SMOKING, SEX, AND POWER

❋

Disclaimer: Make no mistake. I support your right, as an adult, to drink or smoke, if you choose, but I don't believe our children should be drinking, smoking, taking drugs, or having sex. Their young bodies are too vulnerable, their brains aren't fully developed, and their feelings are too tender. If they choose to indulge, they need to make such important decisions based on knowledge and experience, not on adolescent whim, rebellion, or ignorance. While they are young, I do my best to convince them to remain substance-free, so they'll have a better chance of growing up strong and healthy.

Although most effective conversations with students are private, one-on-one discussions, so many students have asked for help with the same problems that I developed five "speeches" that I use to help them handle the temptations they face every day. I thought you might be able to use some of the ideas or phrases from my speeches— feel free to steal a little or a lot. Heck! Memorize them all, if you think it will help a child.

DRUGS

Fortunately, drug-abuse prevention has been incorporated into most school curriculums. Students learn about the negative effects of drugs, their side effects, and the dangers of using them. Unfortunately, so many children think they are immortal, that bad things only happen to other people, that all the statistics and warnings in the world won't keep them away from drugs. They aren't worried about the danger to themselves—for many young people, the danger *appeals* to them.

Through trial and error, I found two things that get the attention of almost all of my students. Instead of talking about the dangers that drug use poses to them, I focus on the dangers to their future children. They may not care about themselves, but they care about those unborn babies. And, instead of warning them about the addictive aspect of drug use, I question why they are taking the easy way out. Here's my Drug Speech:

I want you to know, up front, that if you sell drugs, I have no respect for you. By selling drugs, you are making money from other people's misery and pain, you may be creating crack babies, and you may be responsible for spreading the AIDS virus. If you use drugs, I feel sorry for you, not because you are weak, because nobody is stronger than drugs. I feel sorry for you because you are taking the easy way out. You take drugs because you don't like your life. You want to change your reality, but to change your reality you have to take a good look at yourself, an honest look, and accept responsibility for your life. Then, you have to work hard to change the things you don't like about your life. It's much easier to pop a pill, smoke a joint, take a hit of acid, swallow some PCP or XTC, smoke some crack, stick a needle in your arm, or chew, smoke, or swallow any of the hundreds of drugs people are so happy to sell you. But, as you know, the effects of whatever drug you use are temporary—if it doesn't kill you—and then you come back to reality and it's just the same as you left it. It still stinks. You still hate your life. The only difference is that you have less money now and less time. You've given somebody else your money in exchange for nothing. And you've wasted the most valuable thing you have—your time—because your time is your life. You haven't done a thing to change your reality. It takes a strong person to take on that task, to look himself or herself straight in the eye and take control of life.

The other reason I feel sorry for you if you use drugs is because you may be maiming or killing your unborn children. You all know kids who sit in class and try and try, but they can't learn, and the reason some of them can't learn is because their parents used drugs. I'm not just talking about mothers here. A father's drug use can also affect unborn babies. One of my roommates in the navy had a baby with no arms. The doctors said the baby was deformed because her husband took a lot of acid when he was a kid. He stopped using acid when he grew up, but the genetic damage was done. Maybe the doctors were wrong, but nobody knows for sure. Why take that risk? And if you're thinking, "I just smoke pot, it doesn't cause genetic damage," then you'd better think again. The latest research indicates that marijuana can cause changes in DNA—the stuff that makes up all living things. Every time you experiment with drugs, you are taking a chance with the health, perhaps the life, of your future children. Imagine holding your own baby in your arms, looking into his or her eyes, and telling this innocent child that you're sorry, but you were just "chillin' and kickin' with your friends, having a good time." If you don't like your life, fix it. Drugs can't do that for you.

DRINKING

Many children, particularly teenagers, protest that adults are hypocrites. We are always complaining about their drug use, but then we turn around and drink. They're right. Here's my Drinking Speech:

Lots of you complain that adults are hypocrites because we drink alcohol and then turn around and rag on you about using drugs. Alcohol is a drug, you tell us. You know that because you learned it in Biology or Drug Awareness or Substance Abuse classes. You are absolutely right. Alcohol is a drug, and the reason it is legal is simple—money. Our government makes a lot of money from sales taxes on alcohol. But don't get mad at the government. You've heard about Prohibition, unless you were sleeping in history class. The government tried to make alcohol illegal, but the same situation developed that we have with drugs today. People wanted to drink, so when alcohol became illegal, people made their own and sold it for a lot of money on the street—and they killed each other over it, just the way drug dealers kill each other today.

Alcohol is big business. All those commercials you see with people drinking and laughing and falling madly in love and having a wonderful time are designed for one purpose—to make you spend your money on alcohol. Advertisers aren't interested in whether you become addicted to alcohol. They just want your money.

Money may be the reason alcohol is legal, but it isn't the reason that people want to drink. People drink because alcohol is a drug and people can become addicted to it, just like they can become addicted to any drug. Addiction doesn't have to be physical. Your body doesn't have to crave the drug. Addiction can be psychological. Your brain might need that feeling of release or relaxation or euphoria, or whatever it is you get from drinking. It's easy to tell if you're addicted to alcohol. Stop drinking. If you can't stop, you're addicted. It doesn't matter whether you drink beer or whiskey or drink a six-pack a day or one drink per night or a few every Friday. If you can't stop, you have a problem. Fortunately, it's a problem you can fix. There are plenty of people who will help you, if you can't help yourself.

Regardless of why you drink, or how much you drink, alcohol kills your brain cells. The more you drink, the more dead brain cells. It's pretty simple. If you kill enough brain cells, you kill yourself. Unfortunately, brain cells are the only cells your body can't replace. Once they're gone, they're gone.

The reason I don't think you should drink now, when you're growing up, is because you are growing up. Your body isn't fully developed; neither is your brain. You only get one of each in your life—one body, one brain. Give yourself a chance to grow up healthy, get some more education and experience, before you start taking risks with such valuable assets.

I used to drink a glass of wine with dinner quite often, until I had a roommate who was an alcoholic. She made me see the true nature of the drug. My friend was an intelligent, charming, beautiful young woman when she was sober. When she was drunk, she was nasty, spiteful, and pathetic. I felt so sorry for her. For a year, I picked her up off the living room floor, washed the vomit off her face and out of her hair, and helped her into bed. Then, somebody pointed out that I was helping her be an alcoholic. By taking care of her, waking her up, dressing her, driving her to work on time, I was allowing her to keep drinking. One of the hardest things I've ever done in my life was to tell my friend I wasn't going to help her anymore. Eventually, she admitted she needed help and entered a rehabilitation program. I never saw her again. When she entered the program, she left her old life behind. She never spoke to me again. I hardly ever take a drink anymore, because I remember what it did to my friend and I know that alcohol is much stronger than I am.

I'm not saying that everybody who takes a drink is a drug addict. Adults have a right to drink if they want to, and I stand by their right to drink. But I do insist that we be honest about what drinking is. It's drug use.

SMOKING

Fortunately, children can't turn around today without seeing a poster warning them about the side effects of smoking. Unfortunately, so many adults have stopped smoking that now the cigarette manufacturers are putting even more time and energy into making smokers of children. That makes me very angry. Here's my Smoking Speech:

Do you want to know what makes me mad? It makes me mad that there are hundreds, probably thousands, of adults in this country, who spend their whole working days trying to think of ways to get you to start smoking— and they do this when they know for a fact that smoking will harm you and possibly kill you. They want you to smoke for one reason—they want you to become lifetime smokers, nicotine addicts, so that they can spend your money. They'll use your addiction to pay for their nice clothes, fancy cars, and exotic vacations. That makes me mad and it should make you mad, too.

Smoking looks cool. I admit it. I will also admit that I smoked, briefly, when I was young because I thought it was cool. My brother and his friends used to sneak out to the hayloft in the barn and smoke cigarettes. I wanted to be accepted, and I wanted them to like me, so I smoked with them. The first few times I smoked, it tasted terrible. It made me cough. It made me dizzy, too. It gave me kind of a rush, like spinning too fast on a merry-go-round. After a week or so, I didn't get dizzy, but then I found myself wanting to smoke—I was addicted. Just that fast. Snap.

Nicotine is a highly addictive drug. I didn't know that

then. I didn't know that one cigarette contains one-seventieth ($1/70$) of a drop of nicotinic acid. One drop of nicotinic acid would kill you. So, each time you smoke, you are poisoning your body just a little bit. That's why you get a rush the first few times you smoke, or if you've gone without a cigarette for a long time. Your body is going, "Oh, no! She's poisoning me! What am I gonna do? Let me outta here!" Once you're addicted, you don't feel the rush, but your body still panics and it's still being poisoned.

Fortunately, somebody from the American Cancer Society came to my school a few months after I started smoking. He showed us a piece of a normal lung in a jar. It was pink. It wasn't exactly what I'd call pretty, but it wasn't disgusting. Then he showed us a piece of a smoker's lung. It was black and had crusty little chunks that looked like dirt hanging to it. It made me sick to see what I had been doing to myself. I was committing suicide, one cigarette at a time—and paying a lot of money to do it! Not very smart. So, I quit smoking. I had only been smoking for a couple of months, but I smoked a full pack every day. Quitting was the hardest thing in the world. I thought it would be easy, but I have never been more wrong. I would go for hours without a cigarette, and think I had managed to quit, but then the craving to smoke would overtake me and I would feel like I could kill somebody for a cigarette. I would smoke a butt off the sidewalk if that's all I could find. That was the poison talking.

If you think you can smoke for a while and look cool, and then quit when you're cool enough, look around you. See how many adults are trying to quit—and failing. See how many adults are spending thousands of dollars on nicotine gum, nicotine patches, hypnotism, drugs, and other things to try to cure their addiction. Ask any adult who smokes if he or she has ever tried to quit. The answer will probably be yes. Ask if they were successful—most of them aren't because nicotine is a real killer. Ask yourself if you want to be like them when you grow up, because if you smoke now, you will be like them when you grow up. You'll try to quit. Maybe you'll be one of the lucky ones who does. And you'll try to convince your children not to smoke. I promise you will.

SEX

When I was in high school, about a hundred years ago, nobody admitted to having sex. If anybody at my school was sexually active, boy or girl, he or she lied about it. They didn't want a bad reputation. Ironically, today, half of the boys and girls who boast about their sexual exploits are lying—they don't want anybody to think they're virgins! I make a point of telling my students that it's okay to be a virgin. They need to hear that message from people they trust and respect.

I realize that sex education is a hot point. Who knows whether educating children will encourage them to have sex? We will never know, because people don't tell the truth when they answer surveys about their personal, private lives. They lie for the same reasons that people have always lied about sex—to make themselves look good, whatever "good" happens to be at the time. If people did tell the truth about sex, then I would have met at least one married couple who agree with what the surveys claim is the average number of sexual engagements per week or month. I know an awful lot of married couples, and I haven't met an average couple yet.

Taking a stand on sex education puts us between a rock and a bigger rock. If we don't educate our children and make condoms and counseling available to them because we don't want to encourage them to have sex, will we increase the chances that those same children will end up having babies, getting diseases, or dying from AIDS? That's a question I can't answer. Certainly, parents have a right to educate their children about sex, to discuss their own values and morals, but I also believe that schools have a responsibility to educate children about the facts of sex—because children don't always listen to their parents (and some parents aren't able or willing to discuss sex with their children). I think we have to work together to try to keep our children celibate while they are growing up, but also to protect them if they choose not to be celibate. I don't include discussions about sex in my curriculum, but sometimes the students raise the subject and refuse to let it sit down. When that happens, I give them my Sex Speech:

> You are too young to have sex. You aren't too young to have real feelings. You may be very deeply in love with somebody. I know some couples who fell in love when they were thirteen or fourteen or sixteen years old, and they are still happily married. But I know many more couples who thought they were in love at thirteen or fourteen or sixteen, and ended up with children they couldn't afford and didn't want. If they did get married, they

ended up divorced at a very young age, or very unhappily married at an old age.

I think you are too young to have sex because you don't have the emotional maturity to avoid hurting yourself or other people. Sex is one of the most intimate experiences we humans can share with each other, and when you engage in intimate acts, you make yourself vulnerable to hurt. I'm not talking about physical pain. The body heals. I'm talking about emotional pain. Some people never recover from a broken heart. Don't let anybody talk you into risking your heart until you are ready—ready means grown up and in a stable relationship with somebody you truly know and trust.

When you have sex, you make yourself very vulnerable, physically and emotionally. You know how much it hurts when somebody you trust lies to you or stabs you in the back. That is nothing compared to the pain of giving your heart and body to somebody who tells you they love you, and you find out later that they didn't love you at all. Most of us will have our hearts broken sooner or later, but it's much easier to handle if you're grown up when it happens.

I know some of you have boyfriends and girlfriends who tell you, "If you really loved me, you'd have sex with me." My answer to them would be, "If you really loved me, you wouldn't ask me to do something I don't want to do. People who love you don't hurt you—at least, not on purpose."

Think about this for a minute. Think about who was your best friend five years ago. And think about your favorite hobbies back then. If you had a boyfriend or girlfriend, think about them. Now, do you have the same best friends, hobbies, and boyfriends or girlfriends as you did then? Or have your personality and tastes changed? Well, you're going to keep on changing, for quite a while. Someday you'll look back and see those people you think are sexy—and they probably won't look so good to you. If you still think you love them in a couple of years, you probably do. Wait and see.

Don't confuse sex with love. They are two very different things. If you think that somebody will love you because you have sex with them, ask yourself this: Would you love somebody just because they were willing to have sex with you? There are lots of people in this world who would be willing to have sex with you. Don't look for somebody else to make you feel good about yourself or make you stop feeling lonely. Everybody feels lonely sometimes. That's part of life. If you want to feel good about yourself, do things that make you proud of yourself. Do something good for somebody else. Help somebody who is less fortunate than you are. You'll feel good.

Of course, you think sex is wonderful and magic. It *is* wonderful and magic, but only if you realize that there is a difference between having sex and making love. Anybody can have sex. Big deal. Not everybody can make love. Making love isn't just about making yourself feel good, or making your partner feel good. It isn't just about physical feelings, either. Making love means creating a physical, mental, and emotional bond. That's what makes the magic.

Here's the R-rated version for seniors only—when I know that several students in my class are sexually active:

If you are sexually active and you like having sex because it makes you feel good, or because you want to have an orgasm, then you are using the other person. You are masturbating on somebody else. You might as well just stay home and enjoy your own company—that way you won't get any diseases and you won't make any babies you aren't equipped to raise.

When they giggle and cover their mouths and look at each other aghast because I said the "m" word, I tell them:

You have just proved my point. If you were mature enough to have sex without risking your own or somebody else's emotional well-being, you wouldn't laugh when somebody says masturbation or penis or breast. But you do laugh at those words because you are not mature adults—and you aren't old enough to have sex.

LITTLE SUSIE UTERUS

One year, I had four freshman girls who became pregnant during the school year. These were not wild girls; they didn't drink, take drugs, and party hearty all the time. They were intelligent girls, good students, and nice people. They were also lonely and insecure, and they were willing to do what their boyfriends wanted in return for what they thought was love. One of the girls (I'll call her Darcy) wrote to me in her private journal:

Miss J, you're the only adult I can talk to about this who doesn't yell at me or treat me like a little kid. I know I was stupid to have sex, especially without protection, but I couldn't help it. I said I wasn't going to do it. I prayed in church that I wasn't going to do it. I even told my boyfriend, but then I went right ahead and did it. I wish I knew why I went and did that. Do you know?

I wrote the best explanation I could think of and returned Darcy's journal to her after school the following day. She took the journal, glanced at my answer, and hurried out of the room with it. I thought she was too embarrassed to read it in front of me. Darcy hadn't run from embarrassment—she had rushed to find three of her closest friends. She rushed back into my room with three other girls and directed them to sit down in the front row.

"Tell them the story, Miss J," Darcy insisted. "It's so cool. They have to hear it."

I suggested that Darcy let her friends read what I had written in her journal, but they all begged me to tell them the story. So I did. First, I drew four rows of X's on the white board in front of the room and launched into my Little Susie Uterus speech:

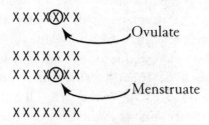

These twenty-eight X's represent the twenty-eight days of your menstrual cycle. At least your cycle is supposed to have twenty-eight days, but we all know that isn't usually the case. Some of us have a period every thirty-two days or every forty-five or every twenty-six days. Sometimes we go twenty-six days one cycle and fifty-three the next, or we skip a period, or have two periods in one month. One thing you can count on, though, is that you will ovulate fourteen days before your period starts. That's when you are fertile. That means you can have a baby. If your periods are irregular, as most of ours are, then you won't know exactly what day you ovulate, but you can bet that the day you ovulate is the day you can't say no. It's the day your body takes over your brain and says, "Shut up. I'm tired of listening to you. You spoil all my fun." And even if you know in your mind and your heart that you don't want to have sex, your body talks you into it. It's your hormones doing the talking, and they are the best saleswomen in the world. "Oh, baby," they say, "just this one time. Please. Please. Please." And because hormones do their best talking on the day you ovulate, you stand a really good chance of getting pregnant. That's why so many girls say, "I only did it once, so how come I got pregnant?" Because the one time you can't resist will be when your body is ready to make a baby. It's biology. It's natural. Your body doesn't know any better. When you start having periods, your body is capable of making a baby, and that's what it wants to do.

And while we're on the subject of periods, let me assure you that they are not nasty, horrible things. They are not a curse, and they don't make you unclean. Having a period is the most natural thing in the world. Here's how it goes. Little Susie Uterus has a nice, cozy little apartment inside you. Just down the street from Susie's place, you have hundreds of tiny eggs in storage. Your body doesn't make a new egg from scratch every month. Your eggs are already there—that's why you have to wear that lead apron if you have an X ray at the dentist's office—so your precious little eggs won't be exposed to X rays that could harm them. So, every twenty-eight days, or whatever your cycle is, one of those little eggs, Ms. Egg, comes to visit Susie. Ms. Egg is lonely. She wants to make a baby. That's her whole purpose in life, but she doesn't have much time. She only has a few hours, a day or two at the most, to wait for Mr. Right to arrive and make the baby. Susie gets so excited about Ms. Egg and her potential baby that she redecorates the whole apartment—puts up new wallpaper, everything. Then they sit and wait. Mr. Right isn't the most good-looking guy in the world. He's a sperm. He's little and wiggly and in a real big hurry. If he shows up, Ms. Egg grabs him, hugs him, and they make a baby.

Usually, Mr. Right doesn't show up. Ms. Egg gets upset and leaves in a huff. Susie Uterus is upset, too, after all that work. So, she rips down the wallpaper and tosses it out—that's the tissue that lines the walls of your uterus. That's your period. Just old wallpaper. No big deal.

Now you know why so many girls get pregnant their first time. Here's my advice. Don't run out and get on the pill. Wait until you are emotionally and financially able to support a baby and give it the best possible life. Instead, avoid situations where you will be tempted to have sex. I'm not telling you not to kiss your boyfriends. It's normal to want to share affection. But don't put yourself in a position where your hormones can talk you into having sex. Don't hang out behind buildings or park in cars or go to parties where there is alcohol or no chaperones. And speaking of alcohol. Remember those eggs? Well, those little eggs are your potential future children. Take care of them. Be good to them. Don't eat too much junk food or drink alcohol or take drugs—because those little eggs eat everything you eat and drink everything you drink. If you drink beer, you are giving those eggs beer. If you take drugs, you are giving them drugs. The stronger you are, the stronger your eggs. Take care of them, so your children will have the best possible chance to be strong and healthy.

Darcy and her friends told the story to their friends, and soon all of my female students were making jokes about wallpaper and Ms. Egg. On Friday afternoons, when the dismissal bell rang, I'd caution the girls: "Have fun this weekend. And, girls, take care of them there eggs." They would laugh, but I knew that they would remember my words when their friends offered them drinks and drugs. Sometimes students ask me, privately, if the damage would be undone if they stopped drinking or taking drugs. I tell them that it would depend upon the quantity and type of drugs they had used, but that the human body is remarkably recuperative and the sooner a woman stops abusing her body, the better chance it will have to heal itself.

POWER PLAY

Every year, in every class, there is at least one student who refuses to play school. He slumps in the back of the room, with his arms crossed, and mimics everything I say, just to see how far he can push before I push back—or if I will push back. She talks nonstop during my lessons, distracts everybody around her, and pitches a fit if I ask her to be quiet because she wasn't doing anything, so why am

I picking on her, I'm the one with the problem. Even worse than those loudmouths are the silent resisters, the ones who refuse to play, and won't talk, either. If you've spent any time at all in the same room, the same house, with an angry child who refuses to talk, you know how loud that silence can be and how much it can affect everybody else in the vicinity.

When I find myself facing a power player, I remind myself that children act like children because that's what they are. They're immature, unreasonable, and aggravating. Sometimes they are so angry they could scream, but they don't know why they are so angry. They just are. I can remember feeling that way as a teenager—I would argue with anybody who told me to do anything, just because. Looking back, I think I was angry because I felt so powerless. People kept treating me as though I were a child, and I thought I was grown up enough to make at least some decisions about my own life.

I remind myself of what it felt like to be so young and insecure that one pimple on my forehead would be enough to make me want to stay home and hide from the world. Then, I give my Power Speech (I'm going to make this a boy speech, but it works equally well with girls):

> You're probably tired of being treated like a child. You aren't a child. You're becoming a young man. You want to make your own decisions, control your own life. But people won't let you run your own life. People keep trying to tell you what to do, what to wear, what to say, what to eat and when to eat it, what to read, where to go and where to sit when you get there, when to go to bed, when to get up, who to be friends with, what to watch on TV, and so forth. I

don't like being told what to do either. And I don't like telling you what to do. I'm not trying to boss you around just
to show that I can. I'm not interested in making you feel
bad. I'm not trying to embarrass or belittle you. I'm trying
to help you become a successful person. I see talent in you
that you can't see yourself, but it's there. I'm trying to help
you find that talent. I want you to be successful in school
and in your job and your personal life. I want you to be a
happy, healthy, responsible adult.

I want to treat you as an adult, but I can't do that if
you continue to act like a child. Adults don't pout when
they have to do something they don't want to do—that's
part of life. We all do things we don't want to do. The
difference between an adult and a child, between a man
and a boy, is that a man accepts things he can't control
and doesn't pout or throw a tantrum. A man doesn't make
life difficult for people who are trying to help him. A man
doesn't have to prove he's tough all the time because he
knows he's strong. He makes choices and he accepts the
responsibilities that go with those choices.

You are not powerless. Nobody can make you do
anything. Think about it. The only things you truly
have to do are eat, drink water, and breathe. The rest is
choice. You may choose to do things because you don't
like the alternatives—if you don't go to school, your
parents may ground you or take away your allowance or
hit you. But they can't make you go to school. You
choose that for yourself. I'm sure you know plenty of
people who cut classes or who don't go to school at all.
As far as that is concerned, you are making better
choices than they are.

Your biggest choice, the most powerful one, is the
choice you make about the kind of person you are. No-

body makes you a liar, a cheater, or a quitter—and nobody makes you be honest or a hard worker or somebody who doesn't give up. You choose those things, too. You choose who you are every second of every day of your life. You can choose to act like a man, or you can choose to act like a little boy.

I am trying to treat you like a man, and I expect you to act like one. That means you don't make my job difficult. You don't fight me just for the sake of fighting somebody—because I'm on your side. If you have an objection—an honest objection—to something I say, or something I ask you to do, then all you have to do is tell me. It's all right to argue, because an argument is just a case of two people discussing different points of view. An argument isn't a fight. There doesn't have to be a winner and a loser. A constructive argument produces two winners—both people learn to see something from somebody else's point of view.

Now, before we go back into that classroom, I'd like to know whether you want me to treat you as a man or as a boy. If you want me to treat you like a man, I want you to look me in the eye and give me your word of honor that you will try to act like one. I don't expect you to be perfect. Everybody makes mistakes. But I do expect you to try. I expect you to treat both of us—you and me—with respect. And I will do the same. I give you my word of honor, and I want you to shake hands with me on that.

I've never had a student who didn't shake my hand. Later, if the bad attitude threatens to visit, I place one hand lightly on the student's shoulder and whisper, "Remember our deal?" They always remember.

Chapter 11

PASS IT ON

❊

Quite often, I used to assign the essay topic *"Why I am the person I am"* to my high school students. When they complained, as they always did, that the assignment was too hard, I would say, "No, it isn't. Don't be so lazy. This is one of the easiest essays you'll ever write. All you have to do is tell me why you are the person you are. Simple."

Last year, I realized just how unsimple that assignment was when I received a letter from a young woman in Ohio. Tawana Washington wrote, "HOW? That was my question I had after reading *My Posse Don't Do Homework*. . . . It seems to me that it was a long road from where you were to where you are, and I'm curious about that journey."

When I sat down and tried to answer Tawana's letter,

I realized I didn't know the answer; I had never had to articulate it. I tried. After five pages, I still didn't know how I arrived at my particular state of personhood, but I felt a little closer to the answer. Wherever I started in my explanation, I always ended with my mother, a born child psychologist and an accomplished armchair philosopher.

A similar situation occurred when I was invited to speak to a group of teachers about my experiences. After my speech, several teachers asked me how I arrived at my approach to education, and where I learned my teaching techniques. Of course, I went to college and took education courses, and observed other teachers, but when I truly thought about it, I realized I hadn't learned as much about teaching from my education courses as I had from my own teachers.

I believe that if you did the same thing—sat down with pen in hand and tried to explain your own philosophy for raising children—I would predict that most of what you believe is based on your own parents and teachers. It is very likely that you will either be following their examples or trying very hard not to follow them. In the future, your own children will do the same.

Tawana's letter and the teachers' questions inspired me to put my thoughts on paper. A five-page outline grew to twenty-five pages, then became a seminar for future teachers (which will become my next book), and the outline for this book. Although I'm not a Ph.D. or a licensed counselor, I do have a degree in psychology, a sizable passel of common sense, and a passionate belief in the inherent goodness of children. Also, I was blessed with a gift for connecting with disenchanted children and motivating those children to succeed in school. I believe that gift was passed on to me by my parents and teachers, and I'd like to share with you the things I learned from those good people. Most of these lessons were taught by positive example, but some were taught by people who inspired me to be as unlike them as possible. How I learned these lessons isn't as important as the fact that they have helped me help so many children. I'm passing them on to you in the hope that they will help you and your child, too. If this book helps even one parent and child connect, it will make my heart sing.

1. Remember that there is a reason for everything a child does.

The reason may not make sense to you, but that doesn't mean it doesn't make sense to your child. Sometimes, when a child makes a mess of things, we ask ourselves, "What in the world was he thinking?" when he wasn't thinking at all—he was simply having fun being a child. When they aren't simply having fun, children tend to operate in three basic modes—angry, afraid, and ignorant. They're mad at the world, they're afraid of the world, or they're misinformed about everything in the world. Figure out why your child is doing whatever he's doing, and your problem is halfway solved.

2. Separate the child from the behavior.

Children (and many adults) believe that when we're angry with them, we no longer love them, or that we love them less when they misbehave. When you tell a child she's a "bad girl," she thinks you mean that she herself is bad. Children not only believe they are what we tell them they are, they think they need to live up to our expectations. If we tell them they are bad or stupid (or good or smart), they will do their best to be those things. We need to make sure that children know we love them in spite of their occasional bad behavior. Hate the behavior; love the child. The message must be clear: "I don't always like the things you say or do, but I always love you."

Even older children tend to believe we stop loving them when they do something wrong. One fifteen-year-old girl called me in the middle of the night once and asked me if I was sleeping. I mumbled, "Yes," and Cristal said, "Never mind. Go back to sleep." I insisted that she tell me why she called. She said she would have to move out of her house because her mother didn't love her anymore. "I told her I had sex with my boyfriend and she started yelling and screaming and now she hates me," Cristal whispered into the phone. I felt like screaming, too, but I forced myself to sound calm. "Naturally, your mother is upset," I said. "Have you ever baby-sat for a small child?" Cristal said she had. "And do you remember how upset and worried you were when that child did something dangerous, like running in front of a car or sticking its finger in a light socket?" Cristal said, of course, she remembered how that felt. "And after the baby scared you, but you found out the baby was all right, then what did you do? I'll bet you yelled, didn't you? You told that baby never to do that again because it had scared you so much." Cristal agreed. "Well, your mother yelled at you because you are her baby. No matter how old you get, you will always be her daughter. You scared her. She's worried about you. It may sound silly, but she yelled at you because she loves you. If she didn't love you, she wouldn't care. Now go talk to her." Cristal rushed into my room the next day, eager to tell me that her mother still loved her.

Don't beat yourself up if you scream or cry or yell when your children scare you half to death. Sometimes panic is a natural reaction. After the tears have dried, remind yourself—and your child—that you can hate the behavior but still love the child.

3. Love them loudly.

Tell your children every single day that you love them. Don't assume they know you love them because you take such good care of them. They need to hear the words. If they blush and stammer, "Aw, gee, Mom," or "Oh, shucks, Dad, stop it," tell them you can't help it, they are so lovable you simply have to tell the world. They may run to their rooms to hide from such mushy nonsense, but they will be smiling as they run.

Show them that you love them by your actions, as well as your words. I can't tell you how many students have written in their private journals, "My parents don't really care what I do. They let me do whatever I want."

Children don't really want to be allowed to do whatever they want. They want you to care about what they do. Unless your child has a legitimate reason why he must stay home, or if she physically resists leaving your house, I would recommend including them in any family outings. If the family is visiting Aunt Betty or Grandma Maudie, then take your child with you, even if he or she complains that it's sooooo boring and wants to stay home. This is a situation where you cannot win. If you insist that your child go along, you'll have to listen to the complaints—

you don't care about his feelings, you're always bossing her around and treating her like a child, you're stopping him from doing his homework so it's your fault if he flunks math, she never gets to do what she wants. If you let your child stay home, you still lose—he will think you don't care about him because if you really cared you would have made him go; she'll wonder whether you secretly wanted to go without her in the first place.

Don't listen to what your child says; listen to what he does. If he complains endlessly, but gets into the car, then he didn't really want to stay home. If you have to physically drag him from his room and force him into the family vehicle, then I would believe he truly wanted to stay home.

"I don't care!" is one of the largest lies that children try to make us believe. They love to tell us they don't care, because they care so very much. If they didn't care, they wouldn't bother to tell us. What they are really saying is, "I don't think you care about me." The louder they shout that they don't care, the more they actually care. When one of my students or stepchildren becomes angry and tells me, "I don't care!" I say, "Oh, yes, you do, because if you didn't care you wouldn't bother to tell me you don't care because you wouldn't care enough to tell me about it." I know that sounds like a mouthful of gobbledygook, but the kids know exactly what I mean.

It isn't the students who complain and argue and whine and protest constantly that worry me, it's the ones who sit in the corner with their arms crossed and their mouths shut and never utter a discouraging word. Those are the students who truly don't care, and they are the most difficult to reach because it takes a lot of pain or anger—or both—for a child to reach that stage. Those are the ones who worry me. I'm not talking here about quiet, shy kids, or ones who would rather listen than talk, or ones who like to think about things for a good long while before they speak. And I'm not talking about kids who are temporarily too angry to talk. I'm talking about kids who shut the door on the world and bolt it behind them.

4. Remember that you aren't supposed to win.
Your job as the parent of a teenager is to be dense and unable to understand the simplest ideas. You will probably outgrow this stupidity within the next fifteen to twenty years and may actually become intelligent. In the meantime, you are extremely embarrassing. Everything about you is wrong—from your dorky hair to your gruesome shoes—and you don't understand an-y-thing.

It's natural for children to separate from their parents at some point during adolescence. They need to begin forming their own opinions, making their own decisions. It's also natural for them to be scared of separating from the safety of constant parental guidance. Some children make the move gracefully, but most of them don't know how to do that, so they pick fights, they create reasons to rebel, they find something wrong with whatever you do or say, to justify going off by themselves. If you keep in mind that they aren't trying to hurt your feelings, and they aren't rejecting you personally, it may make the separation a little easier to accept.

One of the primary joys of childhood is complaining about adults in general, parents in specific. Sometimes children pretend to hate the things they love the most, because of their current view of the world and the way things are supposed to be. When I was fourteen, I remember giving my mother a copy of a very sentimental poem that I had embroidered onto a piece of black velvet cloth. "Don't show this to anybody," I warned her, "because I'm not supposed to like you." I made her wrap it in a brown paper bag and store it on the top shelf of her closet because I liked her so much. I still do.

5. Don't make the unattractive attractive.
The easiest way to make something attractive is to forbid your child to do/eat/watch/read or talk to it. When your child likes something you don't want him to like, whether it's a person, a heavy metal group, or an intergalactic hairstyle, remember that children like to dress up and try things on, including attitudes and people. They usually outgrow their bad taste, unless you try to make them outgrow it. Surely, you remember that from your own childhood.

Children sometimes make their choices to fill certain needs. Hair that covers half a child's face may not be a fashion statement but an attempt to hide from the world or cover acne. A teen who feels unattractive may go out of his way to create an ugly look—an "I wouldn't want to join any club that would have me as a member" statement. A shy child may choose a very aggressive friend because that friend has the strength the shy child wishes she had. A wealthy child may befriend a poor child because he sees the disparity and inequality of their lives and wishes it didn't exist; his friendship may be a way for him to equalize the world.

A child's choice of friends is a major cause of concern for many parents, and rightly so. Friends do have a tremendous influence on each other, but we tend to focus on the child we view as the "negative" one of the pair. We overlook the possibility that the "positive" child may be the stronger influence, that the good student may be trying to help the poor student improve. If your child is very young and chooses inappropriate friends, by all means, intervene. But if you have an older child, especially a teenager, your attempts to pull them apart are much more likely to drive them closer together. The harder you pull, the faster they will run toward each other. Instead of dictating their friendships, try to figure out why your child wants to be with a particular person. What does this person offer your child? Acceptance? Protection from bullies? An entree into the popular crowd? Many times older children will choose to be friends with people they know you don't like, just to establish their independence. Such friendships have nothing to do with friendship and everything to do with showing you who's the boss. When that happens, bite your tongue. I know it hurts, but it's your best bet.

As much as we want to protect our children from harm, we can't. And they don't want us to. A psychologist once suggested to me that the times I have grown the most in my life, and developed what strength of character I have, were the times that I hurt the most. Not much consolation, perhaps, but much truth in that statement.

6. Give kids a chance to back down without losing face.

This is so important, especially with teenage boys who are caught up in the super-macho culture (and more and more girls are following their lead). I would estimate that 90 percent of the fights students have—with other students, with teachers, and with parents—are about dignity and pride, regardless of what the source of the conflict appears to be. From my own experience, the less self-respect a child has, the quicker he is to take offense at what he perceives as a lack of respect from other people.

Even when they achieve a measure of maturity and success, some people remain angry about the lack of respect they felt as youngsters. One of my former students, Alex, who is now a private in the Marine Corps, is a rather tough-looking young man who sports a shaved head and a jacket with the sleeves ripped off. Alex and a fellow marine stopped by my house a few weeks ago to surprise me, but I had recently moved to an address a few blocks away and hadn't yet notified my friends. When Alex stopped at my former residence, my neighbor told him I had moved, so Alex asked for my address. My neighbor said if Alex would give him a number where he could be reached, he would let me know. Alex took offense, stuck his finger in my neighbor's chest, and growled, "You don't understand. Give me her phone number—now!" Later that night, Alex recounted the incident to me. I told him my neighbor had been trying to protect my privacy, but Alex insisted that my privacy was not the issue. "He just didn't think he should have to talk to me," Alex said, flexing his biceps. "He shouldn't have disrespected me like that. I hate it when people do that."

During our conversation, Alex related an incident with his drill sergeant that resulted in a formal reprimand and a reduction in rank for Alex. "I told him I don't care about the money, and I don't care about the stripes. You can take those things away from me, but you can never take my pride." Alex couldn't see that the sergeant wasn't trying to take away his pride. From his limited point of view, everything is measured in degrees of respect and disrespect. Because Alex can't ever back down, he can't move forward.

In order to teach children how to back down gracefully, we need to do it ourselves now and again. If you and your child argue over an issue of independence or freedom or something that won't have a long-term harmful affect, and you sense that your child simply needs to win an argument so he won't feel like a child, then I would consider taking the loss. After you've squared off, argued, and stated your views, give your child a chance to back down gracefully. You might say something such as, "I was not questioning your judgment. I know you have to start making your own choices and dealing with your own mistakes, but I did want you to consider my opinion on this subject. Maybe I'm wrong. I don't know." If you stop there, admitting that you don't know all the answers, you leave the door open for your child to admit the same thing. Often, a child will continue with the behavior in question, just to show he can continue, but will eventually stop it if you ignore it. That way, the choice to stop becomes his. He can say he chose to stop because he wanted to, not because you "bossed him around." He can savor the "respect" you've shown him.

On the other hand, if your child argues with you about something truly important, something that will have a long-term effect on your child's future, then I would recommend standing firm. It is possible for you to lay down the law without belittling your child. One way to do this is to say, "I'm not questioning your judgment, but it's my responsibility to make decisions that affect your well-being and safety. Maybe you are right and I'm wrong. I just don't know, but I have to make what I think is the best decision, and you need to respect my right to make that decision, just as I respect your right to disagree with me. Maybe in a week (or a month or a year), we'll take another look at this situation and see whether things have changed." End of conversation.

7. Accept your responsibilities.

Many children believe that a parent's job is to provide food, clothes, housing, and money, and spoil everybody else's fun. They need to be reminded, frequently, that your true job, as a parent, is to help them grow up healthy and able to function in society. As a parent, our society expects you to do much more than feed, clothe, and house your children—you are also expected to teach them to set priorities, make good decisions, manage time effectively, solve problems, cope with errors, get along with other people, and develop a strong moral character and a solid work ethic. In addition, in your copious spare time, you're supposed to help them with their homework and monitor their education for at least twelve years.

Since one of your primary responsibilities is to see to it that they receive a good education, you aren't being nosy or bossy when you ask questions or involve yourself in your children's education—you are doing your job. We do need to place responsibility squarely on students' shoulders, but that responsibility needs to match their maturity. I think it's unfair to expect students to select their own class schedules until they are seniors in high school. Of course, I think they should be allowed to choose elective classes such as art or music or woodworking, but when it comes to academic subjects, I think parents, counselors, and teachers should select the appropriate courses. If we expect them to learn to challenge themselves, and to become lifelong learners, people who enjoy acquiring new skills and knowledge for its own sake, then we need to teach them to keep setting higher goals for themselves. (Of course, if we expect to motivate them, we also need to make it all right to make mistakes. There is no incentive to try if you are punished for every failure you make along the way to success.)

When my own students want to take the easiest classes or the lightest possible schedule, just so they can have time to hang around with their friends at school, I refuse to let them. I tell them I am willing for them to hate me right now, but that it is my responsibility to make sure they get the best possible education. Many times, students argue that they don't need the credit for a certain class because they aren't going to college. I say, "I know you're old enough to make some decisions for yourself, but because you are young, I am going to make this decision for you. If you decide a year from now, or five years from now, that you want to go to college, you will be prepared and your life will be that much easier. If you never go to college, you will still have a good education. Either way, you win and I will know that I have done my best to be a responsible teacher."

It is your responsibility as well as your right as a parent to know who your child's friends are and how they spend their time together. There is nothing wrong with your calling a friend's parents to make sure there will be a chaperone at a party, or to introduce yourself and ask some questions about the rules at their home. There's nothing wrong with your calling to check on a child who is staying overnight at a friend's house—no matter how old that child is. A sixteen-year-old may be more mature and able to make better decisions than a young child, but the older a child becomes, the more temptations exist and the more pressure there is to give in to them.

Not all parents have the same attitudes and values; children have told me about parents (their own and other people's) who have given them cigarettes, alcohol, or marijuana. One boy told me his father gave him a pack of cigarettes and a beer for his tenth birthday. A mother told me during a conference that she allowed her daughter to have sex at home because then at least she knew where her daughter was and that she was safe. Another mother, whose child was in the same class, told me that she wouldn't permit her daughter to date until she was seventeen.

Talk to the parents of your child's friends. Find out whether you have the same standards of behavior. You may find some parents who think you are overprotective and who prefer to allow their children more freedom. You may not find an ally, but you will have learned quite a bit about your child's friends. When you find parents who share your values and have established a similar set of rules regarding R-rated movies, coed parties, drinking, and so on, encourage those parents to communicate with you about both your children and their activities.

Of course, at some point, you have to let go and hope that you've done all you could as a parent. You and your child are the ones who will have to decide when that time arrives. Until then, do all you can. If your kids protest, tell them it's their job to complain about you and it's your job to spoil all their fun. I like to add, "When you grow up, you can torment your own children on a daily basis. Until then, you're stuck with me, who loves you."

8. Talk. Listen. Talk some more.

The earlier you start to establish a relationship based on mutual respect and communication, the easier your job will be later. If you haven't talked, start now. Tell them you are sorry you haven't talked in the past, but you realize how important it is and you are going to start now. Don't expect immediate results—they usually suspect a trick or some kind of manipulation. They may cross their arms, shake their heads, insist that it's too little, too late, but they probably won't mean it. Children keep people at a distance to protect themselves from being hurt. The more they hurt, the harder they try to protect themselves. Don't push, but be persistent. If you are consistent and keep talking, eventually they will listen. They may act as though they aren't listening, but believe me, they will be listening. If you don't talk, they may translate your silence as "I don't care."

What should you talk about? Everything except the intimate details of your personal life. Talk about politics, your job, who you think will win the Super Bowl, what your boss said at work that made you angry, your opinion about America's involvement in the civil wars of other countries. It doesn't matter what you talk about, and it doesn't matter whether your child agrees with you. What matters is that you talk—and listen.

If your child refuses to talk to you, don't give up. Keep

asking questions. Be prepared to listen whenever the opportunity arises. And when it does arise, try to listen without judging. I know it's hard not to become upset when children do dangerous or foolish things, but if you can manage to remain calm, you have a much better chance of helping them. Be prepared to listen to some ridiculous ideas without laughing, without smiling, without even letting the tiniest little glimmer of a grin show in your eyes—because the first time you laugh at something your child cares deeply about may be the last time you have that opportunity. Instead of criticizing what seems silly to you, ask questions to find out why your child believes the things he does.

Your child may refuse to talk to you, ever, but you can listen to what he or she doesn't say. Children can communicate a world of information without saying a word. In fact, some of their loudest statements are silent. Facial expressions, body language, and the look in a child's eye will tell you much if you pay attention. Sometimes the only response you'll get is a half-second of eye contact in response. You'll have to figure out what that brief connection means.

9. Try to remember your own childhood.
Remind yourself often of how you felt as a child and how huge and overwhelming your feelings were. If you can remember, it will help you understand your own child's behavior and reactions to your behavior. If you can't remember yourself as a child, ask your family and close friends. They'll be happy to remind you of every silly thing you ever did. Surely, you must remember at least one of the following:

- wishing that your parents would stop criticizing your hairstyle, posture, or diction
- wanting to be eighteen or twenty-one so you could be free to live your own life your own way
- worrying that your parents were going to kill you when they found out
- wishing that everybody would just leave you alone for one minute, please!
- being so embarrassed about your pimples that you wanted to stay home and hide
- trying to sit very still so the teacher wouldn't notice you and call on you in class
- wishing with all your heart that a certain person would just notice you
- wondering why you couldn't have had your friend's parents instead of yours
- wearing pants so tight that somebody else had to zip you into them
- wearing an Afro so big people wouldn't sit behind you in the movie theater
- dyeing a white streak across the front of your hair
- wishing you could see your parents at your funeral (wouldn't they be sorry!)
- feeling so mad you could kill somebody because nobody believed you
- wishing your parents would just shut up about your best friend, who was cool
- that sick feeling in your stomach when you know you're going to get spanked later
- wanting to hit your parents

My mother reminded me a few weeks ago that I had once told her I wanted to hit her. I can't imagine my saying such a thing, but I can't imagine my mother lying to me, either, so I will have to assume that I did. "What did you do?" I asked. "Hit me?"

"No," my mother said. "I told you that when you were eighteen, you could hit me if you wanted to. You said, 'Okay. And you're really going to get it. You probably think I'll change my mind, but I won't. I'm gonna hit you good.'"

"I never hit you," I reminded her, lest she forget what a delightful daughter I am.

"Of course you didn't, dear," my mother said, "and I didn't hit my mother, either, although I remember spending many happy hours dreaming about the day when I turned eighteen and could clobber her, because she made the same offer to me when I was a girl."

With practice, if you concentrate, you'll be able to recapture some of the feelings you had as a child. The better you can remember, the better you will be able to understand your own child, because children haven't changed much during the past decades. They aren't so different from you and I when we were children. It's our changed world that makes them seem so different.

10. Be the kind of person you want them to be.
It sounds simple, but it isn't. We give such mixed messages to our children. We tell them to be honest, never to lie, and then we turn around and try to figure out a way to pay less income tax than we're supposed to. We feel justified in our dishonesty because we think the IRS takes too big a bite out of our paychecks, but that doesn't make it any less dishon-

est. To children, issues tend to be black or white, good or bad. They can't see the gray areas, and they pay far more attention to what they see us do than what we tell them to do. If we want them to be honest, compassionate people, we must be honest, compassionate people.

Tell your child at least once a day that he or she is a good person. Remind your child that good grades are not an indication of personal worth. A bad grade can be raised through hard work. When your child fails, don't accuse him of not trying, or tell her she isn't working up to her potential. Ask questions: What seems to be the problem in this class? Why do you think you have this problem? How are you going to solve it? Don't accept "I don't know" as an answer. If your child can't think of an answer, offer one of your own. Do what you would want your boss to do if you made a mess of your work.

Teach your child how to argue. An argument doesn't end in yelling, hitting, or pouting; an argument ends when everybody involved has expressed his or her opinion and tried to convince everybody else to agree. Arguments don't always have clear-cut endings; unlike fights, which have winners and losers, everybody can walk away from an argument feeling like a winner. Maybe your parents didn't know how to argue without fighting, so they didn't teach you, but you can learn and you can teach your child. As a first step, you might tell your child that your parents didn't teach you how to argue effectively, but that you are learning now, at your advanced age, and would like them to learn, too.

Don't lie, threaten, or hit your child unless that's the way you want your child to treat other people, including you. You don't have to tell me how tempting it is to really whack a child. I know how infuriating they can be when they try, and they do try, but physical violence is not an effective way to discourage misbehavior, and it often rebounds. I will never forget my friend Bobby, who always had a nasty bruise or two from his father's beatings. Bobby and his mother both warned his father that what he was doing was wrong, but his father insisted that he was just trying to knock some sense into him. He said it was the only way a stubborn kid like Bobby would learn his lesson. Bobby learned the lesson too well. When he was sixteen, and bigger than his father at last, Bobby broke his father's arm.

One of my students told me that he began doing exactly what he wanted to do as soon as he outweighed his father. "If I want to go out at night, I go out," Rudy said. "He can't do nothing about it or I'll smack him and he knows it. I don't hit my mother, but I don't have to do what she says either. You probably think I used to be a bad kid, but I wasn't. I was real respectful and earned good grades when I was little, but nobody cared, they still knocked me around. Now I do what I want because I know they won't throw me out in the street because they think I'll join a gang or get killed."

Another boy, in the same class as Rudy, explained in his journal why he stayed out of fights at school. "I know my parents worked hard to take care of me and my sisters, and put food on the table and made us a good, clean house, so now I work hard in school and get good grades because I want them to be proud of me. I don't want to let my family down. When people try to make me fight I just tell them, no, that's not the way I was raised. My parents could of hit me, but they didn't even when I was bad. They would just look at me real sad and that hurt me worse, if you know what I mean."

The old adage "We reap what we sow" has always been true, and always will be.

11. Do your homework.

Find a quiet area, a pen, and a piece of paper. Now, think about your own experiences in school, from preschool to college, and jot down quick answers to the following questions. Don't worry, this isn't a test. It's just homework, and homework is meant to reinforce the most important lessons we learned in school and help us put them to practical use.

1. Did you like school, or did you just endure it? Why?
2. How did you handle your homework? (Did you do it immediately? Put it off as long as possible? Copy it? Pretend to have lost it?)
3. What did you like most about school?
4. What did you hate about school?
5. How did you feel when you had to give a speech in front of the class?
6. How did you behave when you were assigned to work on a group project?
7. Did you ever cheat on tests? Why or why not?
8. Did other kids like you? Why or why not?
9. Did you like other kids? Why or why not?
10. How did your parents react to your report cards?
11. How did you react to your parents' reaction to your report cards?

12. What is the worst trouble you ever got into in school?

13. What was the best thing that ever happened in school?

14. Did you play sports or join clubs? Why? Was it as much fun as you expected?

15. Did anybody ever tell you that you weren't working up to your potential? Did you immediately begin working up to your potential?

16. If you had a brother or sister in the same school, did people compare you? How did that make you feel?

17. What did you expect to do after graduation? Is that what you're doing? If not, why not? Are you sorry?

18. If you could go back and change something about your school days, what would you change?

19. If you could thank one teacher, who would it be and what would you say?

20. If you could tell one teacher how wrong he or she was, who would it be and what would you say?

That's it. You don't have to show your answers to anybody, although if you're brave enough, you might show them to your child.

12. Even salty sailors use an SOS now and then.
Don't be too proud to ask for help. Asking for help isn't a sign of weakness or incompetence. It's a sign that you care about your child. In addition to teachers, counselors, classroom aides, and administrators, many schools have social workers or contacts at social service agencies in your

community, such as Big Brothers, Big Sisters, churches, and mental health agencies.

If you have a close friend or relative whose opinion you respect, you may ask him or her to observe you and your child and give you an opinion about why you're having trouble communicating. On occasion, I have asked other teachers to observe my classes and tell me why they think I'm having trouble with a particular student. I'm always surprised when they tell me that it's my own attitude or actions that seem to be causing the problem—but they are often right. Your friends may not be right, but their wrong ideas may put you on the track to the right idea.

Also, ask your friends, relatives, and neighbors to let you know when they see your child doing something wrong. Many adults are reluctant to "tattle" because so many parents become offended or defensive. Let your neighbors know you'd like to know if they see your child smoking, drinking, littering, spraying graffiti, driving recklessly, and so forth. If a child is young, you may want to give other adults permission to discipline or physically restrain your child in an emergency. If we work together, children will view us as a team, and a network of caring adults is more effective than one parent against the world.

WHAT IF NOTHING WORKS?

We do what we can. Sometimes we can't fix things, no matter how much we love our children or how hard we try. Some children seem determined to self-destruct, but as long as they are alive, there is still hope. I didn't make that remark glibly. I've had students who created the worst disasters for themselves, and who refused all offers of help. Some of them grew up to be miserable people, but some of them turned out to be fine, responsible adults. Look around you. You'll see people who drop out of school, become addicted to drugs or alcohol, lose their jobs, go to jail, self-destruct in a thousand different ways—and many of them pull themselves up out of the depths.

I used to become so discouraged and despondent when one of my students dropped out of school, lost a job, or ended up in juvenile hall. Usually, I lose track of the ones who leave, but I never forget them. One particularly unforgettable boy, Julio, told me when he was a high school junior that he expected to go to prison after graduation. There was nothing criminal about Julio. He was a handsome boy with quick wit, a good heart, and an outgoing personality. I asked Julio why he would say such a thing, and he said that most of the men in his family had gone to prison, and so he assumed that he would go, too. I argued that he didn't have to go to prison, but I couldn't make Julio see that he had a choice, and he couldn't make me see that he had none. Eventually, just as he predicted, Julio did go to prison. A couple of years later, another former student called me and said that he had recently seen Julio and that Julio had asked him to let me know that he was out of prison, on probation, and working at a respectable job.

"Julio told me to tell you that he's doing real good, Miss J," Julio's friend said. "He wanted you to know."

I realized then that I had been giving up too soon. Just because a child makes a mess of his life, it doesn't mean there is no hope.

KEEP THE FAITH

Not all of my students had situations as serious as Julio's, but so many of them shared his sense of hopelessness. Every child has his own breaking point, and it's impossible for us to know or predict when that point will be reached. For most students, it takes something drastic to make them give up hope—a divorce or death in the family, a move to a different school, the end of a long-term friendship, failure at a favorite hobby or sport, being ignored or teased by popular classmates. For some students, however, all it takes is a minor obstacle, such as a single low grade on a report card, or simply a general sense of not being as talented or smart as "all the other kids."

Sometimes it is the brightest child who suffers the most. One girl in my sophomore class cried every day for weeks because she had recently moved to the United States and found the language impossible to grasp. In Mexico, she had been a straight-A student and had been used to succeeding in difficult subjects, so her slow progress in English frustrated her. She lost her confidence and abandoned her plans to attend college. Whenever I assigned a one-page essay for homework, Isabel would wait by my desk after class until the other students had left the room. Then, tears in her eyes, she would whisper, "I cannot doing these work, Maestra. I cannot writing one whole page of the notebook. Is too hard for me."

"You are very smart, Isabel," I repeatedly told her. "You can do this work if you try. If you have to write your essay in Spanish and then translate it into English, then you may have the extra time to do that. Someday you will be able to think in English, but that won't happen unless you try. I don't care if it takes you a week to write one page. You must do the assignment."

"Yes, Maestra," Isabel would say each time, and each time she would take her notebook home and write the page. Each time, her writing improved. By the end of her junior year in high school, Isabel was once again earning straight A's, and she received a scholarship from a local college upon graduation. Shortly after she began attending college, Isabel wrote to me. Here is an excerpt from her letter:

Dear Miss Johnson,

How are you? I'm enjoying my life a lot. I'm happy and can't wait to see what's going to happen the next day. I have so many things to tell you that I don't know where to start or if I'll remember them all. I got a computer in a kind of scholarship from my former employer from the job I had during the summer. Isn't it great! And as if that wasn't enough he bought a printer for me (with his own money) so I could print my reports. That's why I'm able to write this letter to you in my new computer and print it on my printer.

...It's fun and at the same time sad to remember all the things that happened during those four years that you were my teacher. Thanks to you I'm able to write this letter in English and be able to go to college. Even though I still have to work on my grammar, spelling, and vocabulary. Please don't ever forget that I love you very much and that even when I don't write you, you're always in my thoughts.

Have fun, enjoy life, and don't ever stop smiling.

With love and lots of hugs,
Isabel Jimenez

One of Isabel's classmates, Johnny, also had a hard time imagining himself as a successful high school graduate, although he had no particular problems in school. Johnny simply didn't see himself as a capable person. Whenever I asked about his plans for his future, Johnny would shrug and say, "I just want to get a good job."

One day, I asked Johnny, "What would you like to be, if you could be anything in the world?"

"An FBI agent," Johnny immediately answered.

"Well, is there any reason why you couldn't be an FBI agent?" I asked. "Are you a dangerous criminal?" Johnny laughed.

"No," he said. "I'm a good kid. You know that." I did know it. Johnny *was* a good kid. He had to work to earn the A's and B's on his report card, but he did his own work. His attendance was perfect, and he was conscientious and responsible.

"Yes, I know you are a good kid," I told Johnny. "And I also know that you can do just about anything you want to in this world if you set reasonable goals and try your best."

Johnny wasn't as easily convinced as Isabel had been. For the rest of his sophomore year, he maintained that becoming an FBI agent was an unreachable goal because it would mean going to college, and he didn't see that in his future.

At that time, I taught in a program where I had the same students for three years, so Johnny couldn't escape my optimism. By the end of his junior year, he began to consider the idea of going to college, and by the end of his senior year, he had decided to attend a local community college. As part of the final exam for my seniors, I

asked them to write an essay explaining the most important things they had learned during high school. One of
the things Johnny said he learned was that he could go to
college. "I never thought of doing that before," he wrote,
"but now I think I can."

It's been three years since Johnny wrote that final essay.
At present, he is working full-time and recently completed
his second year of community college. He is studying
criminal justice and plans to apply for the FBI upon receiving his bachelor's degree.

Johnny and Isabel are only two of many, many examples of students who needed nothing more than somebody
to tell them they could succeed, somebody who believed
in them. They needed somebody to help them create a
vision of success for themselves, and then they went on to
make the vision a reality.

PLANT A SEED

I no longer give up on children. What I try to do, when
I encounter students who have lost hope, is to intervene
in those students' perceptions of themselves as losers.
When somebody fails to make the cheerleading squad,
earns a D in physics, or is rejected by a college admissions
office, I urge him or her to try again or to set a more
realistic goal. I tell them that there is no reason in the
world why they can't succeed if they set reasonable goals,
work hard, and believe in themselves.

Children are no different from adults. If they truly believe there is a chance they will succeed, they will try. But,

if they don't believe there is a chance, whether the obstacles they perceive are real or imagined, they will not try. We can't eliminate failure, and we would be wrong to do so even if we could, because failure so often is a stepping stone to success. What we can do is help children understand *that there is always the possibility of success*, just as there is the possibility of failure. When children believe that it is possible to succeed, they stop being afraid to try.

I tell all of my students that I believe in them, because I do believe, and because I think the most valuable gift an adult can offer a child is hope for the future. I don't expect miracles or quick fixes. I know that it takes time for any seed to flower, but I also know that if you plant a seed of hope in a child's mind, it will grow.

Plant a seed of hope in your child's mind. You may not be present to see it blossom, but it will grow.

RECOMMENDED READING LIST

Recommended reading to get you started. In each book, check the bibliography for more sources of information:

Collins, Marva, and Civia Tamarkin. *Marva Collins' Way*. Los Angeles: J. P. Tarcher, 1990.

Collins, Marva. *Values: Lighting the Candle of Excellence: A Practical Guide for the Family*. Los Angeles: Dove Books, 1996.

Goleman, Daniel. *Emotional Intelligence*. New York: Bantam Books, 1995.

Gordon, Thomas. *P.E.T. Parent Effectiveness Training: The Tested New Way to Raise Responsible Children*. New York: New American Library, 1975.

Holt, John. *How Children Fail*. New York: Delta/Seymour Lawrence Books, 1982.

Holt, John. *How Children Learn*. New York: Delacorte, 1983.

Pipher, Mary, Ph.D. *Reviving Ophelia: Saving the Lives of Adolescent Girls*. New York: Ballantine, 1994.

Rose, Mike. *Possible Lives: The Promise of Public Education in America*. Boston: Houghton Mifflin, 1995.

Sheppard, William C., and Robert H. Willoughby. *Child Behavior: Learning and Development*. Chicago: Rand McNally College Pub., 1975.

Shortz, Will, ed. *Giant Book of Games*. New York: B and P Publishing, 1991.

Steinem, Gloria. *Revolution from Within: A Book of Self-Esteem*. Boston: Little, Brown, 1993.

Wallace, Betty, and William Graves. *Poisoned Apple: How Our Schools' Reliance on the "Bell-Curve" Creates Frustration, Mediocrity, and Failure*. New York: St. Martin's Press, 1995.

The following monthly journals highlight the latest trends and research in education, but are quite "reader friendly." If they are not available at your local public or university library, they may be available on an interlibrary loan from another source. Ask the reference librarian.

American School Board Journal, National School Boards Association, Alexandria, Va.

Educational Leadership, Association for Supervision and Curriculum Development, Alexandria, Va.

Educational Horizons, Pi Lambda Theta, Bloomington, Indiana

Middle School Journal, National Middle School Association, Columbus, Ohio.

Principal, National Association of Elementary School Principals, Alexandria, Va.

T.H.E. Technological Horizons in Education, Tustin, Calif.

Also, if you have a computer, you can check for information on-line via the World Wide Web. For example, I found an interesting article entitled "Research findings show music can enhance key component of human intelligence" at this site: http://gopher.tmn.com:70/0/Artswire/ AMC/MUSBRAIN/rasucher.81594. The home-schooling advocates are quite active on the net and provide a lot of information, as well, that can be useful to parents whose children do attend formal schooling.

Note: It's important to analyze any information you read about children and their behavior, because nobody has all the answers about human development. What is printed in books and magazines is the latest and best of our knowledge, but as my mother used to say: Just because you're right doesn't mean I'm wrong; there can be many right answers to the same question. Feel free to disagree with the "experts." If it works for you and your child, then it works.